PELICAN BOOKS

A 405

MEMORY: FACTS AND FALLACIES

IAN M. L. HUNTER

1962

MEMORY
FACTS AND FALLACIES

Ian M. L. Hunter

PENGUIN BOOKS

Penguin Books Ltd, Harmondsworth, Middlesex
u.s.a.: Penguin Books Inc., 3300 Clipper Mill Road, Baltimore 11, Md
australia: Penguin Books Pty Ltd, 762 Whitehorse Road,
Mitcham, Victoria

—

First published 1957
Reprinted 1958, 1961

—

Copyright © Ian M. L. Hunter, 1957

—

Made and printed in Great Britain
by The Whitefriars Press Ltd
London and Tonbridge

TO

Grace Philp Hunter

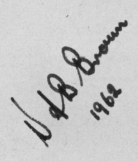

CONTENTS

EDITORIAL FOREWORD

It is easy to get the impression that in Psychology there is little that is firmly established, and that the subject consists in the main of a tissue of highly speculative theories, all extremely controversial and affording no firm basis for confident application. Though the impression is understandable it is quite seriously mistaken. This science resembles a vast territory much of which is covered by a rank growth of exotic weeds, but containing a number of clearings in which good husbandry has produced a number of useful herbs which can be seen growing in neat rows.

An important extension of these clearings, in recent years, has been in the field of 'learning theory'; but there is an allied field which has been well cultivated for more than half a century from which good crops of very saleable produce have been obtained. This is the allied field of memory. Well conducted experiments on the processes of remembering and forgetting have established a number of important facts and exposed an equal number of fallacies.

These facts and these fallacies are the subject of this volume. It is offered to the reader as a reliable, comprehensive, and readable review of our knowledge at the present time.

C. A. Mace

ACKNOWLEDGEMENTS

THE author thanks the following for their courtesy in allowing him to quote from publications of which they hold the copyright: the Editor of the *American Journal of Psychology* for excerpts from papers in volumes 35 and 45 of that periodical; the American Psychological Association for quotations from the *Journal of Abnormal and Social Psychology* and the *Journal of Experimental Psychology;* the Cambridge University Press for an extract from F. C. Bartlett's *Remembering;* the Historical Association for an extract from *Common Errors in Scottish History;* Methuen & Co. Ltd, for a quotation from Woodworth's *Experimental Psychology;* Prentice-Hall, Inc., for an excerpt from H. L. Kingsley's *The Nature and Conditions of Learning;* and the Editor of the *British Journal of Psychology* for quotations from papers in volumes 15 and 32 of that Journal.

CHAPTER ONE

WHAT IS MEMORY?

I

IN everyday speech, we talk of having a good memory, of having a poor memory, of having a better memory for faces than for names, of having a memory that is failing, and so on. Such talk suggests that memory is an object, a thing which we possess in the same way as we possess a head or a big toe. Yet it is true, although alarming, to say that there is no such thing as memory. A big toe can be seen and touched, but not so memory. Should an acquaintance boast of having an excellent memory, we cannot confirm his claim in the same way as if he boasted the possession of a well-stocked library. We cannot ask him to show us his memory. What we could do, however, is to let him read the page of a book, then have him close the book and try to recite what he has just read. If he reels off the page verbatim, we conclude that his claim is, at the least, not without foundation. But we have not observed anything which could be called a memory. We have given him an opportunity to learn something and then to demonstrate how well he remembers it. We have not examined anything which he has, but have watched him doing something, namely, repeating or trying to repeat something he has read. In short, we have concerned ourselves not with an object but with an activity, not with his memory but with his activity of remembering.

Psychology is the study of human activity, of what people do and experience. The key words in its language are words such as talking, laughing, thinking, and striving – transitive verbs descriptive of doing. Such abstract nouns as speech, laughter, and thought have their uses and will be employed in this book. But they also have their dangers. They tempt us back to the sterile faculty psychology of past centuries with its collection of static, lifeless 'powers of the mind', its Perception, Judgement, Memory, Conception, and Moral Taste. And the subject matter of psychology is, by definition, anything but static and lifeless. This substitution of transitive verbs for abstract nouns is no mere verbal quibble. The point simply is that the word Memory, like the word Life, refers not to static entities but to a vast number of interrelated activities or processes. If we are to understand anything of Memory – or of Life – it is these processes which must be studied. The basic memory processes are four in number, namely, learning, remembering, forgetting, and retaining. It is to the introduction of these four processes that this chapter – perhaps the most difficult in the book – is devoted.

Let us start with a concrete example. A schoolboy is given the task of learning a Shakespeare sonnet. He sits down and reads it over several times. Next day in class, he recites the first eight lines without faltering or making a single mistake but, try as he may, he fails to recite the remaining lines. Here we have a complex of processes spanning some twenty-four hours. The first process is that of learning. This is what he is doing while reading and re-reading the sonnet, trying to anticipate which words follow which, going over the difficult parts again and again, and so forth. We, as observers, can to some extent see what he is doing and could, if we wished, check up on his progress by stopping him from time to time and asking him to repeat what he has learned. If we did this, we would find that, as he continued his learning, he would be able to recite progressively more of the sonnet until he could repeat it in its entirety. At this beginning stage, then, the dominant activity is that of learning. The dominant activity on the following day is that of remembering, of reproducing what he has learned. To the extent that he can recite or write out the words of the sonnet, he is remembering. In so far as he cannot reproduce what he learned the night before, he has forgotten. Note that we can observe him in the act of recalling, of saying the words, faltering, filling in the gaps and perhaps correcting himself. But we cannot observe his forgetting: all we can observe is his failure to remember. Last night he could recite the entire sonnet: to-day he cannot. So something must have happened in the interval. And this something is the process of forgetting. The process of retaining, like that of forgetting, is also unobservable. The fact that something can be learned and then, perhaps years afterwards, be remembered means that the effects of learning must have persisted over the interval. This retaining of the effects of learning is carried out by the nervous system. We have no reason to doubt that learning involves some modifications of the nervous system and that these modifications can persist in the form of memory traces. But just what is involved in the laying down and retaining of such traces is something about which, as yet, almost nothing is known. It may be a question of microscopic changes in the actual structure of the nervous system. It may be a matter of purely functional changes such as the setting up of reverberating neural circuits. At present no one knows exactly what is involved. This much, however, is certain: our schoolboy must have retained something of what he learned, otherwise remembering would be out of the question.

In general terms, the above four processes may be characterized as follows. Learning is the process of acquiring some activity or knowledge. Remembering is the process by means of which the effects of past learning manifest themselves in the present. Both of these processes are, to some extent, directly observable. Forgetting cannot be so observed, but its consequence is an inability to remember. Retaining is the brain process by means of which the effects of learning persist through time. All these four processes are intimately related. Thus, remembering and retaining are implicit in learning, for the mere fact that more is known about the poem after a first reading means that the effects of this first reading have been retained and are influencing subsequent readings. Remembering is even more obvious during learning when the boy stops his reading and checks up on his progress by trying to recite what he has already learned. (It will be seen later that such remembering makes a definite contribution to the speed with which learning is accomplished.) Also, no retaining can occur in the absence of learning, for, without learning, there would be nothing to retain. And retaining is a necessary condition for remembering for, without it, there would be nothing to remember. Forgetting and retaining are related, for if there is a failure to retain, then there must be forgetting. It is noteworthy, however, that forgetting can occur without any impairment of retention. The schoolboy may try hard to remember the last line of the sonnet and fail, yet he may, without consulting the original, be able to recite the once forgotten line at some later time. His forgetting did not mean that he had failed to retain the line in question. So, while loss of retention always implies forgetting, forgetting does not necessarily imply loss of retention.

2. RECALLING AND RECOGNIZING

Having introduced the terms learning, remembering, forgetting, and retaining, it is now necessary to say something further about remembering. The reason for this is that remembering may take different forms. In brief, the effects of past learning may manifest themselves through the activities of recall or of recognition: they also manifest themselves by making it easier to relearn the original lesson. Corresponding to these three different forms of remembering, there are three different procedures which may be employed to test for the continued retention of the effects of learning. These are the methods of recall, of recognition, and of relearning. The consequences of using the first two of these methods may now be illustrated by reference to part of a simple experiment conducted by the writer with students taking an introductory course in experimental psychology at Edinburgh University. The method of relearning will be considered in the next section of the present chapter.

In this experiment the students were split up into groups of two, one student acting as experimenter and the other as subject. The experimenter presented his subject with a sheet of paper on which was typed a list of nonsense syllables (more will be said about such syllables in the next section). The list was as follows: TAJ; ZIN; VEC; YOX; FUQ; BIP, DAK; XEW; CUG; JOF. The subject was instructed to memorize these syllables (learn them 'by heart') and was given exactly one minute in which to do so. At the end of the minute, the list was removed and the subject required to show how many of the syllables he could remember. His remembering was investigated in one of two ways, namely, either by the method of recall or the method of recognition. The recall method is straightforward, the subject merely being asked to write out as many of the syllables as he can in any order. The recognition method is a little more complicated because of the necessity of taking guessing into account.

If the original ten syllables are presented and the subject is asked to pick out those which he recognizes, it is possible for even the best-intentioned subject to say that he recognizes certain syllables which, in fact, he does not. When he is in doubt as to whether he really does or does not recognize a syllable, it is difficult for him to avoid guessing. So it is necessary to arrange conditions in such a way that the experimenter can have some indication of whether or not guesswork is involved in the final selection. What the experimenter does is to present an 'identification parade', to give the ten original (or 'old') syllables mixed up with, say, ten 'new' syllables. Suppose this is done and the subject claims to recognize nine of the 'old' and one of the 'new' items. Clearly, the recognition of the 'new' syllable cannot be genuine and must be due to some sort of guessing. And if the subject guesses with regard to a 'new' syllable, may he not also be guessing with regard to one of the 'old' syllables ? With any particular subject, it may be that he does not get one of the original syllables right by guessing, or it may be that, by guessing, he picks out more than one of the 'old' items: we cannot say for certain. But the chances are that if he guesses with regard to one 'new' syllable, he is also guessing with regard to one of the 'old'. If this is so, the number of original syllables genuinely recognized is eight instead of nine. Where there are the same number of 'old' and 'new' items, a subject who is simply guessing has an even chance of selecting correctly or wrongly and, if the number of wrong selections is subtracted from the number of correct selections, his final score will be zero (as it should be since no recognition is involved). In the present experiment, the subject was presented with a list containing the ten original syllables interspersed among twenty 'new' syllables. The recognition list was: YIC; QOM; GEP; FUQ; PAH; XEW; RIJ; NAW; XOL; VEC; DAK; YOX; HUQ; TEF; ZIK; and so on. These thirty syllables were presented and the subject asked to select those items which appeared in the original list. Since his chances of guessing correctly were one in three, the final score was arrived at by giving one mark for each syllable got correct and subtracting a half mark for each syllable got wrong.

Altogether, 104 students acted as subjects in this part of the experiment. Immediately after learning, half of them attempted recall and half attempted recognition. The average recall score was 5·2 syllables, while the average recognition score was 8·3 syllables, i.e. 60 per cent higher. The difference between these scores is such that we can confidently accept a genuine superiority in the recognition performances.

The outcome of the above experiment illustrates the general finding that it is easier to recognize than to recall. Another instance of this finding occurs in the comparison of the traditional-type school examination and the so called new-type exam. The former is exemplified by the question: 'The battle of Hastings was fought in the year—'. Here the examinee is required to recall the missing date. The latter situation involves rephrasing the question thus: 'The battle of Hastings was fought in the year, 1149, 1066, 1035, or 1077'. Here the examinee must recognize one of the dates as being correct. Alternatively, there may be no choice involved, the pupil simply being given the statement that the battle was fought in 1077 and asked to say whether this statement is true or false. Whether the question is of the multiple-choice or true-false type, it is essentially a recognition test. Thus, provided the subject matter permits of such treatment, an examination may be constructed in which some students receive questions demanding recall while others receive exactly the same questions phrased in a way which requires recognition. When this is done, it is consistently found that the final score on recognition questions is higher than on recall questions. This being so, it would obviously be unfair to compare the performance of pupils given a traditional exam with that of pupils given a new-type exam, for the latter would have an unfair advantage. It is of interest, however, that although the pupils' remembering is being assessed in different ways, those who do well on recall also do well on recognition, while those who recall poorly also recognize poorly. This means that if we want to know whether John has learned and can remember more than James, we can use either a recall-type or a recognition-type exam. If John does clearly better than James in the one, he will also do better in the other. Both John and James will do better in a new-type exam than in a traditional exam, but their relative standing will be the same in each.

Instances of the greater ease of recognition as compared with recall abound in everyday life. In the early stages of acquiring language, the young child can understand (recognize) phrases before being able to use (recall) them, and this inability to recall recognizable words occurs even where the child is obviously trying to produce them and has sufficient muscular control to do so. Adults have a similar experience with a not too familiar foreign language. They can give the English equivalent of a French word more readily than the reverse. They can understand the gist of a page of German yet be unable to construct a single German sentence correctly. There is, too, the common belief that people's names are more difficult to remember than their faces. We must all have heard the complaining statement: 'I've got a good memory for faces but I'm poor at remembering names'. As a general statement, this is, at best, a half truth. It owes what validity it has to an ambiguous use of the word 'remembering'. Normally we are required to remember a face when its owner is actually in front of us, walking towards us in the street or sitting near us in the concert hall. And what we do is to recognize the face, that is, react to as being familiar. When, on the other hand, we try to remember a name, it is not usually in front of us at the time. We rarely have the task of recognizing a name; we are most often required to recall it. In so far then as the statement refers to recognizing faces and recalling names, it is true. But if it refers to the recognition (or the recall) of both names and faces, it is undoubtedly not applicable to the majority of people, although there may be a few persons who can both recognize and recall the one better than the other.

The problem of names and faces was put to experimental test in 1934 by an American psychologist, H. M. Clarke. He presented his subjects with a page containing photographs of the faces of twelve men and, under each photograph, a name. The subjects had three minutes in which to study these names and faces by whatever method they would normally use in learning the names of real people. Three minutes later, remembering was tested in four different ways. The original names had to be recognized when mixed up with a number of 'new' names; the original faces had to be recognized from among a number of 'new' faces; the original faces were shown and the appropriate names had to be recalled; and the original names were shown and the corresponding faces recalled. (This last procedure is of doubtful value, since it is difficult to judge from a subject's verbal description of a face just how accurate his recall is.) Nearly 500 college students acted as subjects in this experiment and the results were clear cut. It was easier to recognize names than to recall them; but it was as easy to recognize names as to recognize faces. In so far as it was possible to assess accuracy in recalling faces, this was found to be no better than the recall of names. Thus, on the average, it was as easy to remember names as to remember faces provided remembering took, in both cases, either the form of recognition or of recall; but if either names or faces were to be recalled, the remembering performance was inferior to that involving recognition. In conclusion, the general statement that faces are easier to remember than names is true only if it involves a hidden confusion between recognizing faces and recalling names.

Recollecting. From the examples given above, the difference between recall and recognition should be apparent. We recognize whenever we react to some present experience as being familiar. The sight of a word or a house, the smell of a rose, the sound of a piano, the feel of velvet – all of these may be experienced as being familiar. We recall whenever we recreate or reproduce some past activity or experience. We recall a word by speaking it, or imagining that we see it on a written page, or that we hear it spoken or, if we are blind, that we feel it written in Braille. We also recall past activities when, after a long or short interval, we once more swim, skate, play golf, or drive a car. There is, however, another form of recall which is sufficiently distinct to merit a name of its own. Consider again the schoolboy attempting to recite in class the sonnet he has learned the night before. Not only may he recall the sonnet, but he may recall his learning of it. He may recall sitting down the night before, opening the book, pushing his inquisitive pet cat off the table, reading the poem, watching the sun set, and so on. What is recalled here is located in his personal past and recalling of this sort is termed 'recollecting'. Recreating, in whole or in part, the sonnet and recreating the experiences of learning the sonnet both involve the same basic processes of recall, but they differ in content. We recollect when, for example, we recall our last year's summer holiday or our shopping expedition of yesterday. The distinguishing feature is that the recall of the previous experience involves, at the same time, the relating of this experience to our own past. In company, recollection is usually introduced by the words 'I remember when' and, figuratively, it might be described as a reliving of our past. The mere fact that what is recalled is something which happened to us in the past is, of course, not enough to justify calling it recollection. Our schoolboy may have been told that, at the age of three months, he burned his hand, and he may recall this fact about himself but he cannot actually recollect the happening. Simple recall and recollective recall often go hand in hand, as when we recall a poem and also the occasion on which we last heard it or read it. But simple recall may occur without any recollection: we can all recall the alphabet but few of us can recollect the occasion on which we last recalled it and still fewer can recall being taught it.

Unconscious Plagiarism, Paramnesia, and Déjà vu. Under normal circumstances, recall and recognition are intimately related. Someone points to an acquaintance and asks us for his name. If we are able to recall the name, we recognize it immediately for what it is. Likewise, if we recognize the acquaintance, we are usually able to recall something about him, such as his name, when we last saw him, and his occupation. But recall and recognition do not always go together. There are instances where the one occurs but the other, even with effort, does not. And by their very rarity, these instances arouse our curiosity.

Recall in the absence of recognition occurs in so-called and often unnoticed unconscious plagiarism. There have been a number of famous instances of this in the realms of musical composition, painting, and writing. Here the writer may record a personal experience. He once prepared, wrote out in fair detail, and delivered a lecture on the development of perceiving in children. Later, he chanced to read this lecture over again and was struck by one short passage which was written in a resonant style quite different from all the rest. On considering this stylistic anomaly, he recalled having read something rather similar in Sir James Frazer's book *The Worship of Nature*. He searched through this book and, sure enough, discovered the passage which had been recalled almost word for word in his lecture notes. The writer had recalled a fairly complex passage of some seventy words yet failed completely to recognize it as being other than of his own composition.

Instances of recognition without recall are reflected in the not uncommon remark: 'I'm sure I've seen him somewhere before but I just can't remember where.' Here there is bare recognition, a mere feeling of familiarity unenriched by any subsequent recall; there is the irreducible minimum and the hallmark of recognition, the feeling of having experienced this before. Some more or less well-defined aspect of the present environment (be it a face, or a name, or a building) is referred to our past history but cannot be placed in any adequate setting or localized in time. This whole phenomenon is quite normal and simply shows remembering at its lowest level of functioning. Psychiatrists who have found this effect as a symptom in certain types of mental illness, have given it the name 'paramnesia'. And, for the sake of convenience, we may call the phenomenon by this name even when it occurs under perfectly normal everyday circumstances.

One of the great difficulties facing the psychologist is his lack of control over many of the phenomena he wishes to study. He cannot foretell when someone is next going to experience paramnesia and so he cannot arrange to observe its occurrence at first hand. Even if he is present, it may be impossible for him to say which conditions, both present and past, are contributing to the effect. The psychologist, like any other scientist, prefers to make his observations under controlled conditions, to be able to produce the particular phenomenon at will, and to see what happens when conditions are varied. But is it possible to produce such a fleeting phenomenon as paramnesia under controlled conditions ? In 1941, two Cambridge psychologists showed that it is possible. We may now sketch an outline of this ingenious investigation of H. Bannister and O. L. Zangwill.

Five adults served as subjects; the material consisted of photographs of scenes, objects, and little-known paintings; and the experiment took three days to perform. On the first day, the subject was simply shown a series of six photographs, each photograph being exposed for about half a minute. On the second day, a different series of six cards was used and the subject was hypnotized, that is, induced into a sleep-like state in which he is extremely suggestible. When hypnosis had been carried to a moderate depth, the subject was told that he would be shown a number of cards and would be required to look carefully at each one for half a minute. He was then told to open his eyes and was given the first card to scrutinize. On its removal after thirty seconds, he was given the following suggestion: 'After you wake up, you will have forgotten all about this card, and you will *not* be able to recognize it if it is shown to you to-morrow.' The subject was then shown the remaining cards and, after each, the above suggestion was repeated. At the end of the series, the subject was brought back to his normal waking state. On the third and last day, the subject was tested for recognition, being shown all the photographs used on the two preceding days together with some completely new ones. As each card was presented, the subject was asked to describe whatever came into his mind in connexion with it, what it was like, what it suggested, whether he had seen it before, whether he liked it, and so on. Now, it would be expected that the cards shown on the first day would be recognized as having been seen on that day and that those being shown for the first time would not be recognized at all. This was, in effect, what happened. But how would the subjects react to the cards which had been shown under hypnosis ? If the suggestion that they would be forgotten were accepted completely, then these cards would not be recognized at all. On the other hand, if the suggestion were ineffective, then the cards would, of course, be recognized. The really interesting case would arise where the suggestion was effective only to a certain extent so that forgetting would be apparent without being complete. In fact, three of the five subjects did not forget to a sufficient extent and recognized the cards which had been presented under hypnosis. Two of the subjects, however, showed just the right amount of forgetting for paramnesia to appear. For example, one subject responded to one of the cards as follows. 'I have the impression ... I have the impression that I have seen that before ...' Here he pauses and the experimenter asks if he can remember where he saw it or anything about it. 'I have a feeling I should like to tell you, but why can't I say it ? I have the same feeling as I had ... I know exactly. ... There is something in my mind which is making continual efforts to tell you but my tongue won't get on with the job. Now where did I ? I am just saying to myself now: "Come on, don't be so dumb! You know you have seen it before!" ... It's like making up one's mind to jump over one of those walls that give way under you – those dry walls in Yorkshire – I simply can't give you the answer. It's a very tiring process too.' This subject clearly felt that he had seen the card before but was unable to say when or under what circumstances. These paramnesic responses to the cards showed, in general, three characteristic stages. First, there was the reported feeling of familiarity, the referring of the card to the past. Then followed a strenuous effort to recollect the circumstances under which the card was previously experienced. This effort was found bewildering, rather unpleasant, and exhausting. Lastly, this effort was sometimes concluded by an act of rationalization, that is, by the construction of a fictitious encounter with the card which the subject himself accepted as a genuine recollection. (More will be said about this rationalization process in Chapter Four.) In conclusion, this experiment confirms that paramnesia occurs where forgetting (produced, in this case, experimentally) is almost complete but not quite. It also furnishes first-hand accounts of the way in which people deal with paramnesia, of their tiring and distasteful attempts to recall and, when these attempts fail, of their frequent resort to rationalization.

An experience which is related to paramnesia is that of *déjà vu* (literally 'already seen'). Here there is also recognition accompanied by inability to recall. But in this case, the feeling of familiarity refers to the entire present situation. We have the illusion of having experienced all this before. It is a rather rare experience, but it appears that most people have had it at one time or another. Charles Dickens must have experienced *déjà vu* for, otherwise, he could not have written the following passage in his novel *David Copperfield*.

'If you had not assured us, my dear Copperfield, on the occasion of that agreeable afternoon we had the happiness of passing with you, that D was your favourite letter,' said Mr Micawber, 'I should unquestionably have supposed that A had been so.' On hearing these words, Copperfield suddenly experienced the illusory recognition, which he described with an almost scientific exactitude as follows: 'We have all some experience of a feeling, that comes over us occasionally, of what we are saying and doing having been said and done before, in a remote time – of our having been surrounded dim ages ago, by the same faces, objects, and circumstances – of our knowing perfectly what will be said next, as if we suddenly remembered it! I never had this mysterious impression more strongly in my life, than before he uttered those words.'

In *déjà vu*, whatever is being experienced is, as it were, saturated by the feeling of familiarity. There is the feeling of having already experienced not only what is happening but also that which is going to follow. And this is so in face of the knowledge that we cannot possibly have witnessed the particular happening at some previous time. It is, therefore, quite different from the normal recognition which would occur on seeing a play or film for the second time and is characterized by an uncanny feeling that something is wrong. This whole unpleasant experience normally seems to last for a few minutes at most. Nothing definite is known about the conditions, either in the individual or in the environment, which give rise to it and, in consequence, no satisfactory explanation can be offered. What seems to happen is that the process of recognizing gets, as it were, out of hand, so that, for a short time, anything which occurs is reacted to as being familiar: this distortion has its counterpart in the experience of 'alienation' in which intimately known situations and persons suddenly appear unfamiliar and strange. *Déjà vu* is, incidentally, one of the psychological sources from which the metaphysical doctrines of pre-existence, transmigration of souls, and incarnation may have drawn their inspiration. For if we have the conviction of having already experienced something which we cannot possibly ever have experienced, one possibility is that we have experienced it in some other existence. This is, of course, pure speculation like any of the other attempts to explain either *déjà vu* or alienation. As yet, neither phenomenon is understood. We only know that they occur and represent curious but unexplained relationships between recognizing and recalling.

3. RELEARNING AND SAVING

In the introduction to this chapter, it was mentioned that the effects of learning manifest themselves in three different ways. Two of these were discussed in the previous section. The third way is that learning may make it easier to relearn the same thing – it may produce, on the second learning occasion, a saving in time and effort required to learn. It is this third effect of previous learning which will now be discussed. And there could be no better way of introducing it than by considering the classical work of Ebbinghaus on 'the forgetting curve'.

Although forgetting is a familiar fact of everyday life, it was not until Hermann Ebbinghaus began his investigations in 1879 that it was subjected to systematic experimental study. The results of six years of research were published in 1885 in a book, *Über das Gedächtnis*, which has now become a psychology classic because it records the first application of scientific method to the study of the so-called higher mental processes. Ebbinghaus conducted a number of lengthy experiments and throughout, used only one subject – himself. But, although he assumed the difficult dual role of experimenter and subject, his methods were so thorough that his conclusions have stood the test of repeated re-examination. Duplication of his experiments by later psychologists working in various countries has yielded refined but essentially identical results. The experiment which is of particular relevance here is one in which he attempted to construct a curve of forgetting, i.e. a graph plotting the amount of forgetting against the time which has elapsed since the completion of learning.

The materials he used for his experiments were lists of nonsense syllables. Such a syllable is formed by placing a vowel between two consonants, and examples of it have already been given. His reason for using these artificial syllables was simple. He required lists of material each of which would be equally easy or difficult to learn. Lists of words would not be satisfactory. There are enormous differences in the extent to which words are already familiar to a subject and, also, to which a sequence of words chosen at random form a meaningful phrase for him. One list of words would vary greatly from another in its meaningfulness and consequently, as will be seen in Chapter Two, in the ease with which it can be learned. Lists composed of the rather unfamiliar nonsense syllables tend, on the other hand, to be meaningful to about the same extent. It is true that they neither lack meaning altogether nor fail to vary in meaningfulness from one list to the next. But the extent of this variation is relatively slight, especially if certain technical precautions are taken in preparing the lists.

The procedure used by Ebbinghaus was to learn lists of nonsense syllables, put them aside for an interval, then relearn them and note the saving in time due to the retention of the first learning. During the course of the experiment, he submitted himself to this procedure no fewer than 163 times, and no effort was spared in standardizing the experimental conditions over what must have been a very tiresome many months. Each time, he learned eight thirteen-syllable lists. He took the first list and read it aloud repeatedly at a steady rate of one syllable every 0·4 seconds until a certain learning criterion was reached which, in this case, was two errorless and

unhesitating recitations from memory. After a pause of fifteen
seconds, during which the learning time was recorded, the
second list was learned in the same way to the same criterion.
Then the third list was tackled and so on until all eight lists
had been mastered. The total time required to learn these eight
lists constituted the 'learning time'. After a lapse of from
twenty minutes to one month, the same set of lists were
relearned exactly as before, the time taken to do this being
the 'relearning time'. A measure of the amount of forgetting
was obtained by comparing these two times. If 1,000 seconds
were required for original learning and the relearning took
600 seconds, then the saving was 400 seconds, or 40 per cent
of the original time, while forgetting was responsible for 60 per
cent of the time which had to be spent in relearning. The
general value of this relearning method is that it enables us to
obtain evidence of retention under conditions where neither
recall nor recognition is possible.

There were seven different intervals between learning and
relearning, i.e. 20 minutes, 1 hour, 9 hours, 24 hours, 2 days,
6 days, and 31 days. The results showed that forgetting
occurred rapidly at first and then became progressively
slower. An hour after learning, forgetting was so far advanced
that more than half of the original work had to be done again
before the lists could once more be reproduced. Nine hours
after learning, about two-thirds of the original work had to be
applied. After six days, three-quarters of the original work
had to be repeated and, after a month, some four-fifths. If the
amount of effort saved is plotted against time, a curve emerges
of the type shown in the lower part of Fig. 1. This curve is
familiar to mathematicians as being logarithmic in form. It
falls steeply at first and then continues falling more and more
slowly until a point is reached at which it virtually stops
falling and remains level.

Two points require to be mentioned with regard to this
experiment. The first concerns the use of the relearning method
itself. This method measures not only remembering but
learning ability as well. So if, for any reason, the subject's
learning ability changes between the time of learning and of
relearning, this will influence the amount of saving. Ebbing-

haus, for example, discovered that, because of diurnal variations in his abilities, it took him 12 per cent longer to learn a
list of syllables around seven o'clock in the evening than it did
around ten o'clock in the morning. This meant that, in determining the amount forgotten during a nine-hour interval, the

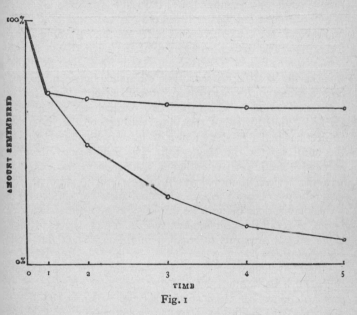

Fig. 1

original learning took place at a favourable time of day,
whereas relearning came at an unfavourable time. And the
fatigue factor would yield a spuriously high amount of forgetting. Accordingly, a deduction of 12 per cent of the relearning time had to be made before calculating the amount of
saving.

The second point applies to the construction of any forgetting curve irrespective of the method by which remembering
is being assessed. It concerns the use of single and successive
tests of remembering. With the single test, a subject or a group
of subjects learns some lesson and is asked to recall, recognize,
or relearn after, say, one hour. If we then want to discover how

much is forgotten in two hours, we must use either another group of subjects or, if we use the same subjects, we must ask them to remember a different lesson. In short, the remembering by a particular subject of a particular lesson is used to determine only one point on the forgetting curve. With successive tests, on the other hand, the same subject is asked to remember the same lesson repeatedly at, say, one hour, two hours, one day, and three days after original learning. The forgetting curve which emerges is of the form shown in the upper part of Fig. 1. Here, the curve falls for a short time and then hardly at all afterwards. The difference between the two curves is due to the fact that, in successive testing, each test is a practice period in which the items remembered are further learned. Thus, after all time intervals except the first, the subject has had a greater amount of learning practice than has the subject with the single test. The facilitating effect of successive testing on retention is analogous to the value of periodic review in formal study or teaching. A student, for example, who hears a lecture and must answer questions on it a week later, does better if he thinks over the lecture each day trying to recall the points made and the topics discussed than if he merely attempts to recall it in the exam without such previous review.

Other psychologists have repeated Ebbinghaus' experiment. They have used nonsense syllables, passages of prose, geometrical figures, and a host of other types of material. They have used the methods of recall, of recognition, and of re-learning. And they have uniformly found that, under everyday conditions, forgetting occurs more rapidly at first and more and more slowly thereafter. So uniform has been this finding that Ebbinghaus' logarithmic curve has been called by some *the* curve of forgetting. This is, however, an overstatement of the case, since not all forgetting conforms to this curve. The curve may even be induced to rise rather than fall, for conditions can be arranged so that someone will remember less immediately after learning than he will at some later time. The crux of the matter is that remembering is a complex process influenced by a wide variety of factors which do not remain constant from one remembering task to another. This

being so, we could hardly expect forgetting to run a mathematically uniform course even though the forgetting curve is
logarithmic under the majority of circumstances. It is, rather,
to the conditions affecting remembering that we should turn
our attention. These conditions fall into three broad categories:
those operating at the time of learning; those operating during
the retention interval; and those operating at the time of
remembering. The next chapter will be devoted to a discussion of the first such set of factors.

4. THE DEVELOPMENT OF REMEMBERING

In the preceding sections, the various modes of remembering
were characterized as they manifest themselves in adult human
beings. It was seen that remembering occurred in the execu-
tion of learned performances, in recognition, in recall, and in
recollection. Here, we turn to remembering as it occurs in
young children. The intellectual processes of the young child
are, of course, particularly difficult to study since he has no
equipment with which to tell us what he is thinking. He is not
yet able to speak or draw or write. Nevertheless, it is possible
by careful, critical, and prolonged observation of his activities
to discover a great deal about the ways in which he learns, sees
the world around him, remembers, thinks, and so on. Of the
psychologists who have made and interpreted such observations, the most notable have been Professor Jean Piaget of
Geneva and the late Professor William Stern of Hamburg.
They have revealed much about the intellectual processes of
children and, in so doing, have thrown light on these same and
related processes as they occur in adults. For one thing, they
have demonstrated that even the most mundane processes
which we take so much for granted are, in a very real sense,
achievements which owe their existence to a lengthy period
of early learning. That this is true of our ability to use language
is obvious to anyone who comes into even casual contact with
the developing child. What is not so apparent is that such
seemingly *a priori* achievements as being able to see a stable,
meaningful, three-dimensional world around us, to conceive
of time, weight, quantity, and volume, must also be acquired

through learning – as must also our ability to look back on our own past. For another thing, these studies show that our present intellectual abilities do not all make their appearance at the same time: some emerge early in life, while others must await a later level of development. This means that it is justifiable to speak of some processes as being 'higher' or 'lower' than others in that they are characteristic of a more mature or less mature stage of development.

The development of remembering has received most attention from William Stern, who gives a short and very readable account of his conclusions in a book entitled *Psychology of Early Childhood* (1924). He demonstrates that there is, over the years, a gradual growth of remembering abilities and, from his observations, it seems possible to distinguish three broad stages of development. In the first stage, remembering shows itself in the modification of the child's behaviour: his activities are permeated by the effects of previous experience, but these effects are bound to the present and the child cannot yet look back on his past. In the second stage, certain situations elicit recall of events which were earlier experienced in those situations and, as the child grows older, he is able to recall events which occurred further and further back in the past. In the third stage, he becomes able to refer these recalled experiences to a definite past time: this ability does not develop to its full extent until after the child is of school age.

These stages may now be discussed in more detail but, first, it must be emphasized that they do not represent hard and fast categories. They do not attach to any specific age level, for some children develop more rapidly than others. Nor do they reflect mutually exclusive states, for the child does not suddenly jump from one stage to the next. They represent nothing more than a general trend in a continuous and extremely complex development.

Stage One. A craftsman takes a block of wood and carves it to resemble a figure. He then stops carving, his knife rusts, and he himself ages and dies. But the effect of his carving persists because the wood is now of a different shape than it was before. Now, this is, in a very broad and primitive sense, an instance of remembering. In this sense, remembering means simply that the condition of the individual, at any moment, is influenced by previous occurrences which, although past, have not been altogether abolished with the past but continue to operate into the present. In this primitive sense of historical conditioning, remembering is, of course, not unique to human beings, since it occurs also in the lower animals, in plants, and in non-living objects. But primitive though this form of remembering is, it is far from being unimportant. Consider a young child of eight months or so. At this moment, he is what he is because of his past history. He is plump or emaciated in consequence of the quality and quantity of the food he has had; he is sunburnt or pale in consequence of having been in the sun or indoors; his eyes are blue or brown in consequence of his having this or that background of heredity. Any occurence may leave behind effects which are very different in nature from that of the occurrence itself. But the effects are left nonetheless. Notice, however, that in this primitive form of remembering, there is no question of looking back into the past or (to express it more accurately) of constructing, out of the retained effects, the nature of the original occurrence. There is, at this level, only a past history which has vanished, leaving its accumulated effects on the present condition of the person, animal, plant, or object. The same is true when we turn to the lowlier forms of learning.

Consider again our eight-months-old child. Not only does he show the effects of previous nutrition, exposure to sunlight, and so on, but he shows the effects of his own previous activities, i.e. the effects of learning. For example, he recognizes certain people and objects as being familiar, he executes co-ordinated movements of which he was formerly incapable, and he has acquired some routine habits. He has, in short, profited much from his past experiences. Probably as early as his second month of life he would have begun to greet the appearance of his mother's face and voice with a faint smile. And around the third month he would have begun to react to strangers in one way and to members of the immediate family in another. Again, he would, for example, have developed a co-ordination between the use of his eyes and his hands and his mouth. According to the observations of Professor Piaget, there is, by the third month, no reciprocal interaction between grasping, sucking, and looking. The mouth sucks the hands but the hands to not try to carry to the mouth everything they grasp; nor do the hands attempt to grasp everything that the mouth sucks; and the eyes look at the hands but the hands do not try to feel or to grasp everything the eyes see. Gradually, as a consequence of continual exploration and experimenting, the child achieves a co-ordination between grasping and sucking. The hand grasps objects which it carries to the mouth and, reciprocally, the hand takes hold of objects which the mouth sucks. Looking is not yet co-ordinated with grasping, for the child grasps objects only when he touches them by chance. But soon he begins to grasp objects which he sees and not only those which he touches or sucks. However, he still only attempts to grasp when the hand and the object are together at the same time in his field of vision; neither the sight of the object alone nor of the hand alone leads to grasping. Somewhere around the age of six months, the child grasps what he sees without limitations relating to the position of the hand. An object presented to the eyes is now grasped even though the hands are not in his field of vision to start with: likewise an object discovered by the hand outside the visual field is brought into the field of vision. He has now developed a co-ordination between grasping, sucking, and looking which, however modest in comparison with the much greater achievements of the adult, is nonetheless a remarkable accomplishment.

A detailed observation of the activity of the eight-months-old child reveals that it is permeated through and through with the effects of his past activities. Not only does he recognize certain people and objects and possess certain motor co-ordinations which he lacked before, but he has acquired certain routine habits and has even become sufficiently acquainted with the pattern of recurrent activities to be able to anticipate, in a rudimentary way, what is to follow. For example, starting at the age of three and a half months, an infant was given broth from a spoon once a day as she lay on her mother's lap. At first, it was difficult to get her to hold her face up and, after each spoonful, she turned her face to one side as she had been accustomed to do at her mother's breast. After four weeks, however, she had gradually adjusted to the new way of feeding, for she now held her head straight and often even parted her lips before the spoon actually touched them.

Thus we see that, even in the child of a few months, past experiences have already exerted a profound effect on his present activities. But all these effects are bound to the immediate present. In this respect, the child's remembering is, despite its greater complexity, on a level with the remembering of the carving by the block of wood, since neither he nor the wood show any indication of being able to reinstate the vanished past occurrences. There is no indication that, while lying awake and alone in his perambulator, he pictures to himself his mother's face, or imagines the sound of her voice, the soothing feel of her hand, the appearance of his feeding-bottle or of his rattle. There is, in other words, no indication that he can reinstate in the here and now that which is not here and now. The child seems, as yet, to have no acquaintance with his past. He owes, it is true, all his knowledge and his capabilities to this past and its after-effects, but he cannot look back on it.

Stage Two. The earliest signs of recall occur sometime about the completion of the first year. The one-year-old child has, for example, often been observed to leave a ball or toy lying out of sight in some unusual place, such as under a piece of furniture, and, perhaps as long as fifteen minutes later, make his way straight to where it is hidden on being asked to fetch it. Delayed performances of this sort suggest that recalling is involved. These early indications of recall are often reintegrative in character, that is, the child finds himself once more in some situation which elicits recall of something which was previously a part of that situation but is now absent. Thus, Stern reports the case of a boy of nineteen months who once saw bacon being fried and called an onion which was thrown into the pan a 'ball'. Two weeks later, bacon was being fried again and the boy, on seeing the pan, exclaimed

'Da, mama ball ba!'. Another boy of twenty-three months recalled an experience which had occurred ten weeks before. He heard his sister mention 'board' and at once pointed to an easel-board and said 'wow-wow'. There was no dog drawn on the board but, ten weeks before, his mother had sketched there the large heads of a dog, a horse, and a cat, much to the boy's delight. To be sure that his remark was really a question of recall, his mother asked what else he had seen on the board, to which the boy replied 'gee-gee'. In the ten-week interval, there had been no drawings on the board and the boy had been away from home for a period. Such instances of recall are, however, by no means frequent even in the third year of life, and it still seems to be largely a question of 'out of sight out of mind'.

In the fourth year, recalling is more frequent and even occurs a year after the original experience. Infrequently recurring situations, such as summer holidays and Christmas parties, elicit recall of the same situation a year before. Thus, one boy of three years and three months went for his summer holidays to a mountain resort and recalled events which had taken place in this resort on the previous year. He recalled, for example, that an aunt had lived in a certain room and that a man had jokingly threatened him in a particular restaurant because he would not eat. In the fifth year, recalling is more frequent still and there are several reported instances of some chance incident eliciting recall of an experience which occurred more than half a lifetime ago and which has never been repeated or even mentioned in the interval. At this age, it might be said that the child can recall the events of his youth. From now on his recalling becomes less exclusively dependent on reintegration. It becomes increasingly spontaneous in that he reinstates earlier experiences which are not associated with the situation he is in at the moment or with the questions he is now being asked. As he grows older, his recalling becomes increasingly facile and selective. He recalls those past experiences which will assist him in solving some present problem; he even combines the recalled experiences of events which happened at different times in very different places and produces out of them experiences which have no equivalent in direct perception of the real world. At this point, his activities of recalling merge into those of thinking and imagination and, in his mental life, he gains freedom from the restrictions of present time and space.

Stage Three. The observations of Stern and others suggest that the performance of recollecting is not achieved until early in the second year of life and does not appear with any great frequency until around the age of three. But even when experiences are recalled, there is little question of their being referred to any definite point of past time for the simple reason that the child has yet to develop a clear notion of time. Even the four-year-old has little more than an indefinite notion of 'long ago' and a broad distinction between 'earlier' and 'later'. He cannot refer an event to 'the day before yesterday' or to 'last week' with any probability of accuracy. And temporal localization in terms of months or years is more than the child's necessarily limited past experience will permit. Sometimes he can accurately locate a recalled experience as having happened 'today' or 'not today', but he can scarcely use 'yesterday' as a more exact location for experiences from the less immediate past. So far as he is capable of making temporal distinctions between his recollected experiences, he does so by reference to places. 'That was at so-and-so's house' or 'That was at such-and-such a town'. He may even give the impression of a definite time-index, as when he says that a certain event occurred at Christmas or at his birthday. But it seems unlikely that these expressions reflect any definite notion of temporal sequence. He simply seems to place one event in the context of a more outstanding event which is recollected without any clear reference to its location in a temporal order of events. It would appear that he is in much the same position regarding the days, weeks, and months as are most of us regarding the eras of prehistory. Certainly, it is not until later that the child develops even a sketchy notion of having left a portion of his life behind and it is not until after the age of six years that he acquires an awareness of his own past as a historical sequence of events.

In summary of this introductory chapter, it may be said that memory is neither an object nor a faculty but is, like life, a complex of interrelated processes. In outline, these processes involve the modification of the individual by some occurrence (learning), the persistence of this modification during some latent period (retaining), and the manifestation of this modification in some later activity (remembering). At its lowest level, remembering is intimately bound up with the present ongoing activities of the individual: it shows itself in the executing of learned habits and in recognizing. At a higher level, remembering involves the reinstatement of activities and, especially, of experiences which are not part of the here and now. This is recall, and means that, out of the presently retained effects of a past occurrence, the individual can, in some mysterious way, produce a replica of this occurrence. At a higher level still, the individual is capable of recollecting, that is, of not only reinstating past occurrences but also referring them more or less accurately to some period in his own personal history. Consciously, he is able to experience a past which is, in actuality, dead and gone. Where an individual remembers something at one time but, at a later time, cannot repeat this remembering performance, forgetting is said to have taken place.

CHAPTER TWO

MEMORIZING

I

BECAUSE of its literal and repetitive characteristics, memorizing is, despite its complexity, one of the easiest forms of learning to consider and investigate. It is the purpose of this chapter to discuss memorizing with a view to making clear the significance of the learning process for memory in general. Memorizing is the name given to what is popularly called 'learning by heart', and we are all familiar with the process, for we employ it whenever we set out to learn by rote a poem, or a speech, or a list of dates. It is characteristic of memorizing that it leads, if successful, to a literal reproduction of the material. This literal aspect is a distinguishing feature between memorizing and 'content learning' such as occurs when we listen to a story or witness some happening. When asked to recall a story or a lecture or a book, we are quite satisfied if we can give the gist of the matter and outline the main events in our own words. But we are discontented with our memorizing of a poem unless we can repeat it verbatim in the words of the original. It is also characteristic of memorizing that it involves repeatedly going over what is to be memorized. It is true that we can often repeat a strange name, a telephone number, or a particular expression in a foreign tongue after only a single reading or hearing. But such learning is usually fairly superficial and is soon forgotten. Certainly it is insufficient for the mastery of a short poem or passage of prose: these have to be read or heard several times before they can be reproduced.

Especially in adults, memorizing tends to be a deliberate systematic activity undertaken with the explicit intention of being able to reproduce the given matter with the greatest possible exactness. So often is this the case that it might be tempting to regard memorizing as being exclusively voluntary to nature. However, material may also be memorized 'incidentally' in the absence of any deliberate intention of doing so. This 'incidental' memorizing is particularly evident in the pre-school child. From about the age of three years, the child memorizes poems and jingles and the words of dancing games. Yet he does not deliberately set himself to do so, and indeed is not capable of considering any task systematically and of continually repeating it with the intention of mastering it. At this age, intentional learning is, at most, evident only where it is a question of acquiring certain gymnastic feats which seem desirable at the moment. After hearing a little verse once or twice, he tries to join in. He appears unable to listen passively and all that he hears must at once be repeated by his own lips. When he hears the verse once more, he tries to copy the recital regardless of the fact that the words may mean nothing to him, that he omits many of them, says some of them wrongly, and is always some little distance behind the reciter. But with each repetition, he takes renewed delight in the rhythmic, euphonic, reduplicated sounds and soon becomes word (or rather sound) perfect. It would be untrue to say that his imitative vocal activities are not motivated but it seems certain that he does not deliberately set out to learn. He lives too much in the present to undertake explicitly the acquisition of a performance which is to be used only in the future. His memorizing of the jingles is a by-product of his delight in producing the sounds themselves. Other instances of 'incidental' memorizing occur in both adults and children in sufficient numbers to show that deliberateness is, although helpful, not an essential characteristic of memorizing. Learning 'by heart' may or may not be intentional.

In the previous chapter, it was pointed out that the relationship between learning and remembering was an intimate one. In general, it can be said that the better the original learning, the better will be the subsequent remembering and, by inference, the retaining. This statement has such a wealth of evidence in its support that it has become axiomatic. Just what it implies is perhaps best made clear by reference to another of Ebbinghaus' experiments.

Ebbinghaus asked: What happens if the number of learning trials given to a particular list is either less than or greater than that required to reach the criterion of two errorless recalls? In other words, if, for a particular list, twelve trials are required to reach the criterion, what would happen if he took, say, twenty-four trials or only six? In an attempt to answer this question, he conducted tests in each of which syllable lists were read attentively a given number of times which varied, from test to test, between eight and sixty-four. Then a day later, he applied his usual relearning method to determine the amount of saving. He found that the surplus repetitions were not wasted. Even though the immediate effect – a smooth and errorless recall – was not affected, overlearning made for the improvement of later recall. The longer he studied, the more he remembered and the less he forgot. Even original practice which was insufficient for immediate recall was not without effect since it made subsequent learning easier. Ebbinghaus described these results figuratively by saying that each repetition engraved the series more and more deeply on the nervous system. Later investigators confirmed these results and extended them by showing that each learning trial does not result in a constant amount of saving. The increase in remembering which results from an increasing number of repetitions shows a diminishing return. To illustrate this, we may cite some of the results obtained in 1929 by W. Krueger working in Chicago. His experiment was carefully executed and elaborately designed to test the issue in question, but it will suffice to give only a brief sketch of his procedure.

Krueger had three groups of subjects learn a list of twelve nouns. The first group were given repeated learning trials and stopped after their first errorless recitation. The second group also learned up to this point but had, in addition, half as many trials again. The third group was taken to the point of one perfect recitation and then given as many overlearning trials again. Thus, if a subject required ten trials to reach the criterion, he would be given ten trials in Group I, fifteen in Group II, and twenty in Group III. After an interval which varied from one to twenty-eight days, each subject was required to relearn the original list under conditions which yielded both a recall score and a saving score. Examples of those scores were as follows.

	GROUP I	GROUP II	GROUP III
Per cent saving after 1 day	21·7	36·2	47·1
Per cent saving after 28 days	1·5	20·5	25·1
Per cent words recalled after 1 day	3·1	4·6	5·8
Per cent words recalled after 28 days	0·0	0·3	0·4

These figures show that the amount remembered increases with an increase in the number of learning trials. But increasing the number of trials from, say, ten to fifteen results in a greater improvement than an increase from fifteen to twenty trials. Incidentally, these figures also show that the relearning method provides a much more sensitive measure of remembering than does the recall method.

There is, in summary, a uniformly positive relation between amount of practice and the amount remembered, with diminishing returns at the higher degrees of learning. Thus, a student who wants to be sure of remembering a lesson would not stop studying at the moment when he had just mastered it. He would overlearn by continuing his study a little longer. He would, however, be unwise to continue overlearning for too long because, after a time, the additional effort involved would not justify the progressively more minute gains in later remembering.

The above discussion shows that the greater the degree of learning (in terms of the amount of learning practice), then the better is the subsequent remembering. This finding has enormous practical implications for those who want to know how they can 'improve their memory' since it gives rise to the following sound advice: if something is to be remembered, make sure that it is thoroughly learned in the first instance. However, if this advice is to be of use, it is necessary to understand something of the learning process itself, to know something of the variables which affect it, and to discover the conditions under which efficient learning occurs. The variables affecting learning can be grouped under three broad headings. First, the nature of the material learned (or *what* is learned). Second, the conditions of practice under which learning takes place (or *how* learning is conducted). And third, the personal characteristics of the learner (or *who* does the learning). It would be impossible to give an account of everything that is known about these variables but an attempt can be made, in this chapter, to describe a few of the most important ones which fall under each heading.

2. THE NATURE OF THE MATERIAL

It is obvious from our everyday lives that the ease with which something is learned depends greatly on what is to be learned and how much of it there is. A number of interesting variables arises here. As regards the quality of the material, the outstanding variable is that of meaningfulness. As regards the quantity of the material, there is the question of the maximum amount which can be learned in a single trial: this is the classical problem of the 'memory span'. Then, too, what happens as the amount of material is increased ? If we can learn ten lines of a poem in six minutes, how long will it take us to learn twenty lines ? Will it be just twice as long, or will it be less than twelve minutes, or will it be more ? Let us now examine each of these variables in turn.

Meaningfulness. Consider the following three lists of material. (1) TAS - YAL - DOP - SIW - MEL - YOS - HIW - LON - MAF - GIW - NAL - WOH. (2) WAS - TIN - LAY - WHY - OLD - WOE - NIL - LOW - HAM - FIG - MOP - ASS. (3) WE - ALL - SAW - A - TINY - GOLD - FISH - WHO - SWAM - IN - MY - POOL. No experimental investigation is required to tell us that these lists would not be equally easy to learn. We would have to read through the first list several times before we could recall it. The second list would be recalled after a smaller number of readings. And the third list would be reproduced after no more than two readings. If we ask our subject why he found one list easier to learn than another, he would reply that the lists varied in meaningfulness. The second list is easier than the first because it contains familiar, though unrelated, words and the third list is easier still because the words hang together in a sentence, they 'make sense'. This exemplifies, in an obvious way, the rule that ease of learning is directly dependent on the meaningfulness of the material for the subject. Indeed, it would be surprising if this rule did not hold, since meaning implies previous learning. To someone who has never learned to read, the above three lists would all be equally difficult to learn, for they each contain exactly the same letters. Even the letters themselves would appear as just so many marks on paper in the same way as Chinese characters appear to us. As our illiterate person learns to read, these letters become progressively more meaningful, that is, he can recognize them, pronounce them, and recall a variety of things about them. And as with the letters, so too with their arrangement into words and with the arrangement of words into phrase sequences. As he reads and speaks more and more, he learns (although he may not be aware of it) that certain sequences of words occur more frequently than others; he becomes familiar with the statistical structure of the English language.* In short, material is meaningful for a particular person to the extent that it has been involved in his previous learning. Thus, to say that the material is meaningful is to imply that the person has already learned something about it even before being shown it on the present occasion. It implies that he is not being asked to learn something new 'from scratch' but that, in a very real sense, he is merely having to relearn something which he has, in part, learned before. We find this with complex material. The more familiar we are with a science or a foreign language, the easier it is for us to learn more about it, such as a new law or a new idiom. And when we come to consider mnemonic systems and devices, we will see that one sure way to ease the learning task is to use 'recoding', to rearrange the material into a more familiar and meaningful form. The three lists given above exemplify this 'recoding' technique, for the differences between them lie not in the letters themselves but in the way they are arranged and grouped.

Amount of Material. 'It is obvious that there is a limit to the power of reproducing sounds accurately. Anyone can say *Bo*

* This rather abstruse point about the statistical structure of language is lucidly discussed in G. A. Miller's book *Language and Communication* (McGraw-Hill, 1951).

after once hearing it: but few would catch the name of the Greek statesman M. Papamichalopoulos without the need of a repetition.' It was with these words that J. Jacobs, a British psychologist, introduced, in 1887, the first experimental study of 'memory span'. The span is the name given to the maximum amount of material which can be 'grasped' (recalled immediately) after a single presentation. Now, this, like the great majority of psychological performances, is variable rather than constant. The same person may, at one time, correctly recall a list of eight digits yet, at another time, be unable to do so. This does not mean that the amount recalled is unpredictable but it does warn against facile pronouncements concerning a person's span based on but a few tests. It also means that to get a really accurate measure of an individual's span, he must be given a large number of tests and the results of these tests must be treated in a special statistical fashion. However, those psychologists who have most occasion to estimate memory span – the administerers of 'intelligence tests' – cannot spare the time required for a precise estimation, and contrive to use an approximation which involves much less effort. The method is simple. The experimenter has a number of standard lists of, say, digits which vary in length from two digits to ten digits, e.g. 39418, or 4538217069. There are two or three different lists of each length and the subject is told: 'I am going to say numbers and, when I have finished, I want you to repeat the numbers in the same order.' Starting with one of the shortest lists, the experimenter reads it out at a uniform rate of one digit per second and the subject must try to repeat this list. Progressively longer lists are then given until a length of list is reached on which there is complete failure. The span is taken as the longest list ever repeated correctly. Memory span determined in this way agrees fairly closely with that determined by more time-consuming methods, except that it tends to be slightly lower than the latter.

For adults and children of various ages, the memory span has been found for a variety of different materials. Some average results for University students are as follows: digits = 8·5; consonants and differently coloured cards = 7·5; common nouns and simple geometrical figures = 6·0; pairs of common words, nonsense syllables, and short simple sentences = 3·0. All these values, as we can see, are characteristically small. Even with such a simple aspect of memorizing as the memory span, it is found that a large number of variables are at work in influencing a person's performance. The span varies slightly with the rate at which the items are presented and is increased if the material is presented rhythmically rather than at a steady rate. Span is impaired by fatigue, there being evidence to suggest that, with school children and students, it shortens slightly but fairly steadily as the working day progresses from morning to evening. Span is also impaired by distraction, the drinking of alcohol, and the smoking of tobacco (at least in those not accustomed to smoking). Quite the most interesting of the variables affecting span are those which are a function of the individual. These will be discussed later in the present chapter.

If an individual learns three nonsense syllables in one reading or hearing of three seconds' duration, how many readings will he require to learn six syllables ? It might be expected that he would take just twice as long, that is, six seconds. In fact, this expectation is not borne out, for some four or five readings will be required. In one study designed to investigate the relation between amount of material and the time required to memorize, different lengths of syllable lists were presented to adult subjects. Lists of 12, 24, 48, 100, 200, and 300 nonsense syllables required, on the average 1·5, 5, 14, 37, 93, and 195 minutes for learning to a criterion of one errorless recall. These typical figures show that, as the amount of material increases, learning time not only increases but increases by a disproportionate amount. It takes more than twice as long to learn 24 as to learn 12 syllables, or to learn 200 as to learn 100. Where lists of nonsense syllables are concerned, a fairly general finding is that the time-per-syllable increases in proportion to the square root of the number of syllables in the list: lists which are shorter than the memory span are, of course, exceptions to the general finding. This rule also applies, though not quite so generally, to the learning of meaningful material such as prose or poetry. It is true that, with such material, exceptions occur where a longish passage is learned in as few readings as a shorter one. But on he whole, the time to learn increases disproportionately to the length of the passage. Thus, in one typical experiment, prose passages were memorized. A passage of 100 words required 9 minutes, one of 200 words required 24 minutes, one of 500 required 65 minutes, and one of 1,000 required 165 minutes. In conclusion, then, it is generally true to say that the more there is of any type of verbal material, the more difficult will it be to memorize and that, if the amount is doubled, trebled, etc., it will take more than twice, three times, etc., as long to master it.

3. THE CHARACTERISTICS OF THE LEARNER

One of the most fascinating and perplexing aspects of any psychological process is that it differs from one person to another. It is a truism that each individual is unique, and many mistakes and harsh judgements have been made by ignoring that this is so. But this does not mean that individuals do not have certain characteristics in common; the bulk of this book is devoted to such general processes as people share with each other. Nor does it mean that this very uniqueness of the individual cannot be studied. He is unique by virtue of his social upbringing, his schooling, his sex, his age, his genetic inheritance, and so on. And it is possible to examine each of those conditions in relative isolation from the others and discover the contribution which it makes to the person as he now is. Such an investigation is, of course, difficult and complex, but psychologists have shown that, with regard to certain variables at least, it can be carried out. The variables to be considered here are those of motivational state, sex, age, and intelligence. The secondary but none the less important question will then be discussed: do fast learners remember better than slow learners?

Motivational State. The same individual does not learn with uniform efficiency at all times. His learning performance varies with his condition at the time of learning. Strong emotional excitement, fatigue, illness, and drugs all serve to impair his learning along with his psychological functioning in general. Another condition which exerts a profound influence on learning as such is that of being motivated. It is true to say that the best, if not perhaps all, learning is motivated. Without an intention to learn, little worthwhile learning occurs. This truth may be borne in on the school teacher who reads out a short poem several times to his class so that they can learn it verbatim and is then shocked to discover that he cannot recite it himself after the children are able to do so perfectly. The child listens with the intent to learn what he hears, while the teacher has no such intention. Just exactly what is involved in being motivated in general or in having an intention to learn some specific lesson or item of information is something which psychologists have not yet begun really to understand. But we all of us know the difference between being motivated towards some goal and not being motivated. And we also know that such a state of being motivated is distinctly helpful to learning. The student will recollect that on those occasions when he 'couldn't work up any enthusiasm' for study it was hardly worth his while carrying on. Teachers, too, are aware of the beneficial effects of getting their pupils interested in the lesson, of making them want to learn more about it. We learn those things which interest us and fail to learn what does not. Someone who claims to be 'just no good' with car repairing or carpentry usually means that he has never been sufficiently interested in these activities to learn the necessary skills and knowledge. He is probably capable of doing carpentry; what he lacks is interest. People who come into the psychology laboratory to participate in a learning experiment usually come with an intent to learn. This intention may be the result of curiosity, interest in the subject matter, or a desire to please the experimenter and, in most learning experiments, an adequate intention to learn can be established simply by means of giving instructions. It can also, if necessary, be strengthened by the skilful use of various positive and negative incentives such as the giving of money rewards or of praise or of reproof, or the encouraging of rivalry between individuals or between groups.

Sex. Are men better learners than women or *vice versa?* The most general valid answer to this question is: neither. Many investigations have been carried out in which male and female subjects have been given identical learning tasks under the same conditions. Sometimes the women have done better than the men, sometimes the men have done better than the women, and, most often, they have done equally well. In short, no consistent differences have emerged between the sexes. Such differences as have emerged can be ascribed to differences in training and interest rather than to any basic differences in learning abilities. Men may be better at learning to deal with mechanical problems. Women may do better with material which relates to home life. But this does not reflect a basic difference, for if the task is robbed of those features which make it appeal more to one sex than to the other, then differences in learning disappear. With nonsense syllables, for example, we find nothing other than random differences between the sexes. As regards learning and remembering, the difference between men and women is comparable to the difference between, say, a gardener and a mechanic who would differ in their learning of this or that type of task not because of any basic unalterable differences in ability but because of differences in their interests and their familiarity with the terms and the skill being used.

Age. The relationship between age and learning has been most adequately explored with regard to the memory span for digits auditorily presented. The reason for this is that the last twenty years have seen at least three really large-scale investigations concerned with the devising of intelligence tests for practical application in education and industry. Each of these scales has been standardized on thousands of subjects carefully selected, at every age, to be representative of the population at large. And each scale employs, as one of its many items, a test of auditory digit span. According to the published norms of these tests, children have average memory spans of 2, 3, 4, 5, and 6 digits at the ages of $2\frac{1}{2}$, 3, $4\frac{1}{2}$, 7, and 10 years respectively. Thus, there is a steady but progressively diminishing increase in span with increasing age. This increase continues more and more slowly until the span reaches a steady average value of about 7 digits between the middle teens and 30 years. (Note that the average digit span for University students, as cited in the previous section, is about 1·5 digits higher than the average for the population at large.) Then, somewhere about the age of 30, the span begins to decline slightly. The rate of this decrease is nothing like so rapid as the initial rate of increase in the very early years. But a fall is clearly present, for, by the middle 50s, the average span has shrunk to 6 digits, that is, to the level of the 10 year old. Thus, learning performance in the simple memory span situation increases in the early years at a rate which parallels that of physical growth to level out at about the age of physical maturity; and after the age of 30, it shows a slight but definite and progressive decline.

The above conclusion regarding the relationship between age and auditory digit span is well established. However, there are no researches which enable us to draw comparable conclusions for any other learning performances. The absence of such researches is due, in part, to the difficulties attendant on any large-scale survey, namely, those of obtaining and testing a large and truly representative sample of the total population. An even greater difficulty is that age, as it is said, does not come alone but brings with it variations in a number of factors which are difficult to distentangle from 'pure learning ability'. Older people become more skilful in attacking problems of the type which has become familiar to them over the years, and they may acquire a number of learning tricks such as will be discussed in the chapter on mnemonic systems. On the other hand, older people may 'get out of practice' and perform poorly in the formal type of learning situation which school-children and students are accustomed to meet every day. They may also be unprepared to exert themselves in mastering what is, to them, a silly and unprofitable task. In face of these difficulties it is, at the present time, impossible for the psychologist to make definitive pronouncements on the relation between learning and age. The consensus of contemporary opinion seems to be that: where the task is relatively unfamiliar to people of all ages (as is the case with memorizing digits and nonsense syllables), ease of learning increases rapidly in the early years, levels out in the late teens, and falls off gradually after the age of about thirty; where the task is one in which past learning is likely to improve present learning efficiency (as in the mastery of relationships and ideas) then ease of learning may continue to improve for much longer and not decline, if at all, until much later in life. (It is obvious, of course, that in senility the learning of anything at all undergoes impairment if it does not become downright impossible.) The great likelihood of this relatively early falling off of learning efficiency is something which may be unpleasant for those of us who are past the first flush of youth. But it need not depress us unduly, for, though we may not be able to learn as quickly as our younger selves, our general level of performance is probably better than it was because of our greater fund of both general and specialized knowledge. A lawyer in his sixties may be a slower learner than he was at the age of thirty, but he is, nonetheless, likely to do better in his professional work because of having the accumulated experiences of thirty additional years.

Intelligence. Whenever a person's learning efficiency is compared with his performance on a test of general intelligence, the relation between the two is found to be high. Nor is it surprising that this should be so. A test of general intelligence is a standardized method of interview which presents the interviewee with a large selection of problems. These problems are chosen so as to be representative of the various problems which any of us are likely to meet in the course of daily life within a particular society. How well we do on these problems is, therefore, a reflection of how well we have learned to cope with everyday problems in the past. It is also, and here lies the value of the test, an indication of how well we will learn to deal with future problems. Those who score high on the test are those who have profited most from their past experiences and who will also be successful in handling new learning situations. Thus, an intelligence test measures, in large part, simply our ability to learn. Little wonder then that the test score should tend to correlate highly with a particular example of the individual's learning efficiency.

Do Fast Learners Remember Better? There is a popular notion that speed of learning is related negatively to the amount remembered. The learning of the bright student who acquires knowledge with ease and speed is felt to be unstable: easy come, easy go. The dullard, on the other hand, may have to toil long and hard at his learning task, but he is thought to have learned it well: slow but sure. Now, in one respect, this notion is correct for, other things being equal, the less time spent in study, the poorer will be the learning and subsequent remembering. The slow student who works at his lesson until he is more than thoroughly familiar with every aspect of it, remembers more than his faster colleague who barely masters it and no more. Longer practice, as has been seen, is rewarded by better remembering. But what happens if the fast learner and the slow learner have the same number of practice trials, the same amount of time in which to learn ? The fast learner learns more and, in consequence, remembers better. When the time allowed for learning is held constant, the slow learner is at a disadvantage because of his slowness and the fast learner gains an advantage from his superior speed. This relationship also holds, though to a less striking extent, when the slow learner and the fast learner are equated in terms of the criterion to which learning is carried, e.g. if they are both allowed to continue to the point where they give their first perfect recitation. Even here, the fast learner demonstrates a slight superiority in later remembering. At first sight, this finding seems to contradict the axiom that learning and remembering are closely related, for surely if the two learners have the same degree of initial mastery they should, on a later occasion, remember equally well. The fact is that, on detailed analysis of the two learning performances, it is found that when learning is carried to the same criterion, the faster learner has actually learned better than the slow learner. To understand just why this should be so would involve us in a lengthy and technical discussion which would be out of place in a book of this sort. (The psychologist reader is referred to a difficult but penetrating article published in 1954 by B. J. Underwood in *The Psychological Bulletin*.) The main findings can, however, be summarized as follows. First, where fast and slow learners are carefully equated for degree of learning (a complex procedure which can only be carried out mathematically), then there is no difference whatever in their later remembering performances. This is, of course, a mere restatement of the maxim that the amount remembered depends directly on the degree of original learning. Second, where fast and slow learners are given the same time in which to learn or, to a lesser extent, are allowed to continue until they have reached the same learning criterion, then the fast learner remembers better than the slow learner. However we look at it, the slow learner has to expend more learning effort in order to compete with the remembering performance of the fast learner. He is handicapped from the start. This handicap can, of course, be overcome in many instances, for the slow but diligent learner may eventually learn more than his faster but more indolent fellow.

4. THE CONDITIONS OF PRACTICE

The speed and efficiency of learning depends not only on the nature of what is to be learned or on the abilities and states of the learner. It depends also on the way in which the learning task is tackled. Is it, for example, better to learn something all at one sitting or to study for several short periods with other activities interspersed between work sessions? Is it better to learn a task as a whole or to split it into parts and learn each part before proceeding to the next? The central question running through this section is: What is the best way to set about learning? It must be stated at the outset that there exists no straightforward answer. There is no one optimal method of work. What is best for one task may not be so for another, and the optimal approach varies not only from individual to individual but also in the same individual from one time to another. In any practical situation, the psychologist must discover what the optimal method of learning is in much the same way as the general medical practitioner must discover the most suitable method of treating any particular patient. And like the medical man, the psychologist is aided in his discovery by a number of generalizations which have been established through patient investigation. Some of these generalizations may now be considered as they apply to recitation, whole learning, and distributed practice.

Recitation. In memorizing any sort of material which is later to be reproduced, the effectiveness of repeated reading, listening, or looking is enhanced by recitation, that is, by attempts at recall introduced during the actual learning session. This point can be illustrated by another experiment conducted by the writer, for demonstration purposes, with a class of first-year University students.

EG.

Each student in the group was given a printed selection from Mrs Browning's poem *Aurora Leigh*. The selection contained 112 words and 16 lines with each line numbered in sequence. He was given exactly five minutes in which to attempt to memorize the selection and told that, afterwards, he would be asked for an accurate recall, i.e. he must write out the correct words in their proper sequence and in their appropriate lines. The time given was long enough to enable every student to master a fair proportion of the poem but not sufficiently long to enable any, except a very few, to master it completely. Half of the students were to use recitation and the other half were not. Those using non-recitation were instructed as follows. 'Begin at the first line and read through the material to the end. Then read the material through repeatedly from beginning to end. Keep your eyes on the printed material at all times and make no attempt to recite or anticipate what comes next. Work as quickly as possible.' The other half of the students were instructed in recitation. 'For the first minute, read the material through from beginning to end as in the non-recitation method. Then, when I give the signal, begin recitation. Read a line, then close your eyes and try to repeat it silently to yourself. If you cannot repeat it, read it again and, if necessary, again. Then read the next line, close your eyes, try to recall it, check if necessary, and go on to the next line again. Work as quickly as possible and don't waste time trying to recall lines which you obviously haven't yet mastered.' After these instructions were given, each student spent five minutes in memorizing and then spent a further five minutes trying to write out as much as he could recall. He then scored his recall by counting up the total number of words correctly reproduced. Over a number of different class sessions, 150 students acted as subjects in this experiment, half of them using recitation and the other half non-recitation. Those using recitation recalled, on the average, forty-six words while those not using recitation had an average recall score of only thirty-three words. Thus, the best learning was obtained by those who devoted a large share of their time to recitation. Other investigations show that, as expected, the superiority of the recitation group is still present when remembering is tested for not immediately after learning but some considerable time later.

A large number of studies have agreed in finding that reading plus recitation makes for better learning and remembering than does reading alone. Why should this be ? In the first place, recitation arouses the active participation of the learner and so lessens the possibility of continued inattentive and unprofitable re-reading. Second, it provides knowledge of results, letting the learner know what he has accomplished so far and where he must concentrate his efforts: it also gives him the motivational stimulus of trying to improve his own record. Lastly, recitation provides a direct preparation for later recalling. By reciting, the learner performs just those activities which will be required of him later. There is an often ignored difference between the activity of reading something with a view to learning it and the activity of actually recalling what has been learned. A student, for example, does better in exams if he practises writing out specimen answers than if he merely confines himself to understanding, no matter how thoroughly, the material of his study.

Whole versus Part Learning. In the whole method, a speech or poem is read through and through from beginning to end until it is mastered. By the part method, the material is divided into sections and each section is memorized separately before trying to recite the whole. Which method is the more economical ?

A consideration of the time relations involved may clarify the difference between these two approaches. Suppose a twelve-line poem is to be memorized. It might be learned as a whole or in three parts of four lines each. We have already seen that the whole would require more than three times as long to learn as any one third by itself. So it would take a shorter time to learn three separate thirds of the poem than to learn the whole. But once the parts have been mastered, there still remains the task of combining them together. And this apparently simple task may take a considerable amount of time not only because the sequence of the parts must be learned but also because there will have been some forgetting of the earlier parts during the learning of the later sections. Therefore, depending on the time required for combining the parts, the advantage of the shorter time-per-unit inherent in the part method may or may not be lost.

In addition to this time factor, the two methods also involve different ways of organizing the material. An advantage accrues to the whole method in that it enables the learner to get a general impression of the task before him. This is particularly so with meaningful verbal material. In the case of the twelve-line poem, there may be a meaningful unity about the whole which is lacking in the parts. Thus, learning is facilitated to the extent that the whole method enables the learner to grasp the development of the parts within the general outline of the whole.

Bearing in mind these temporal and qualitative differences between the two methods, it is not surprising to find that the whole method is most effective with relatively small amounts of material, while large amounts of material cannot be handled adequately except by the part method, especially where there are parts which are more clearly integrated within themselves than is the whole. An important factor in determining which method will be most effective is that of the learner's attitude towards the method employed. This effect of attitude is well expressed by a quotation from the book *The Nature and Conditions of Learning* by H. L. Kingsley.

Children often prefer the part method, and unpractised adults are often skeptical of the advantages of the whole method. With the whole method much more time and work is required before any results of learning are manifest. One may read a long poem through a dozen times without being able to recite a single line, while with the same amount of work by the part method the learner would probably be able to recite several stanzas. For this reason a learner gets the feeling of success sooner with the part method. The recitation of parts become sub-goals, which provide a series of steps toward the main goal, the ability to recite the whole. These intermediate goals and the satisfactions derived from reaching them no doubt favour the part method, particularly with children and with adults unaccustomed to rote memory work. The whole method is likely to be discouraging because the learner has to work so long before he can see any returns for his effort. He may feel that he is not making any progress or that he is wasting his time with this 'new-fangled method'. This attitude operates against the success of the method. The experienced and informed learner knows that the readings in the whole method are not a waste of time. He knows, as Ebbinghaus demonstrated, that every reading yields an increment of learning, which is spread over the whole, and that if he continues, he will eventually find the whole selection rising above the threshold of recall. He knows that while he must work longer before results are manifest, the final returns fully justify his patience and endurance.

This attitude factor is probably responsible for the finding that sometimes the advantages of the whole method does not appear at first but only emerges after the learner has acquired experience of and confidence in the use of this procedure.

In very general terms, it can be said that whole learning is best with good and experienced learners and comparatively small amounts of material. With very large amounts of material and inexperienced or poor learners, the part method is best, parts being selected which are the largest the learner can grasp as a meaningful unit. With a moderate amount of material, the best plan seems to be the flexible one of starting with the whole method and keeping a watch for any difficult parts which may have to be given special attention.

Spaced versus Massed Practice. Ever since the issue of distributed practice was first raised by Ebbinghaus, experimental psychologists have agreed that, in general, it is better to have several short learning sessions spaced out at intervals than to have one long unbroken period of work. The sort of investigation which gives rise to this agreement is that published in 1940 by an American psychologist, A. P. Bumstead. Bumstead, like Ebbinghaus, used only himself as subject, although most experimenters have employed groups of subjects, either school-children or students. In one session, he would read a fifty-line excerpt from Milton's *Paradise Lost*, beginning at the first line and reading through to the end at his normal reading speed. In each successive session, he would repeat this process, trying to anticipate what came next and prompting himself from the text whenever his recall faltered. These sessions continued until he could recite the whole passage without referring to the text. Altogether, he memorized nine such fifty-line selections with each session spaced at intervals which varied from one hour to eight days. The results showed that increasing the interval between memorizing sessions progressively reduced the time actually devoted to memorizing. When sessions were spaced at one-hour intervals (in the daytime only), forty-three readings were required involving a study time of 140 minutes. When sessions were spaced at one-day intervals, the number of readings required was only nineteen with an actual study time of sixty minutes. With eight-day spacing, the readings dropped to thirteen and the study time to forty-six minutes. Now, these rather typical results reveal that the greater the spacing, the smaller is the amount of time spent in actual study, while, of course, the total time required increases. This means that spacing can only be profitably used where there is a lengthy time available for study, and the problem is how best to distribute this time among a number of learning activities. Spacing would be of little use to a student 'cramming' for an exam.

Apart from giving the opportunity for additional and perhaps surreptitious practice, moderate spacing appears to owe its general superiority to a number of different factors which are not quite fully understood as yet. Broadly speaking, these factors are of the inhibitory and interfering kind from which the learner can only recover by giving up his specific learning task and doing something else.

In deciding how to distribute practice in any practical

learning situation, we are faced with the double problem of discovering the optimal length of the practice period and the optimal length of the interval in terms of the total amount of time available for study. As regards the practice period, it would seem that it should be short but not so short that the learner has no time to 'warm up', to 'get into the swing' of the task. With more difficult tasks, with younger and more inexperienced learners, and in the earlier stages of learning, the practice period should be shorter than with easy tasks, mature learners, and tasks which are in an advanced stage of practice. The reason for this is simple. The more difficult the task, the more fatiguing it is; and the same task is more difficult for young children, for people unaccustomed to concentrated learning, and for people for whom the specific task is unfamiliar. As regards the length of the interval between sessions, little of a general nature can be said since the optimum depends on the nature of the task, the characteristics of the learner, the stage of mastery of the task, and also the nature of the activities engaged in during the 'rest' interval. All that can be said is that if the task is relatively easy or short, then no distribution of practice will be necessary at all. If the task is difficult or long, then practice should be spaced in such a way that the learner will not have time to lose interest in the work or forget too much of what he has already learned.

General Rules for Directing Memorizing. It might be thought that such learning hints as have been given in this section are disappointingly vague. If so, it must be reiterated that learning is a complex affair (if it were simple, we would have understood it long ago) and that it is impossible to hand out neatly-packaged, all-purpose recipes which can be applied to any learner in any and every learning situation. The psychologist is better equipped to advise on the method of learning when he knows the concrete conditions under which that learning is to take place. He must be cautious if he is to avoid the dangers and distrust which will surely result from the over-hasty generalization of one or two empirical findings. The following guides may, however, be used provided the variability of the memorizing process is kept in mind along with its dependence

on the age and intelligence of the learner, his previous learning
experiences, and the nature of the task.

1. Secure and maintain motivation to learn by providing
   appropriate incentives.
2. Utilize existing motivation by integrating the task into
   activities which are already interesting.
3. Items to be remembered together and in sequence should
   be presented together and in that sequence.
4. Use the whole method for short, easy lessons and a
   combination of the whole and part methods for longer,
   more difficult lessons, giving special attention to difficult
   parts.
5. Insure accurate first impressions, avoiding errors if
   possible and correcting them on their first appearance.
6. Use early recitation, but not so early as to encourage
   guessing errors.
7. Make the material as meaningful and as rhythmic as
   possible.
8. Distribute practice, making memory drills short and
   stopping at the first sign of fatigue.
9. After learning, insure adequate overlearning directly by
   reviewing frequently at first and, later, at progressively
   longer intervals.
10. After learning, insure adequate overlearning indirectly by
    integrating what has been learned into further activities.

CHAPTER THREE

WHY DO WE FORGET?

I

IN general, the events of yesterday can be recalled more vividly that those of a week ago, while the happenings of some years back are often completely beyond our ability to recall. In the absence of periodic rehearsal, the effects of past learning fade with the passing of time. Everyone knows, even without recourse to the psychologist's forgetting curves, that forgetting and time go hand in hand. And if it be asked why we forget, the obvious answer seems to be that we do so because of time. But this explanation, despite its apparent reasonableness, is completely unsatisfactory because time is not a causal agent. Iron rusts in time and children grow in time. But it is not time which is responsible for both. What is responsible is, rather, a number of chemical and physical changes. These changes require time for their completion but are not the consequences of time as such. In short, time enters as a factor not in its own right but merely because it permits a number of effective variables to operate. No chemist would be satisfied with the answer that iron rusts because of time. He would insist that it rusts because of oxidation. So, too, no psychologist would ascribe forgetting to the passing of time. He also would point out that it occurs because time has permitted a number of factors to show their effects. And it is these factors which he proposes to study in the same way as the chemist studies the conditions responsible for the oxidation of iron or the physiologist studies the nutritional and metabolic factors at work in the growing child.

If the above denunciation of time as a cause of forgetting seems rather abstruse, it may be mentioned that there is a further objection, namely, that time by itself cannot account for every change in the effects of past learning. It has already been mentioned in passing that there exist circumstances under which the inverse of forgetting occurs. In these rare cases, more can be remembered at some later time than can be remembered shortly after the original experience, so that the passing of time is accompanied by an improvement rather than by an impairment in remembering (such paradoxical improvement is referred to as 'reminiscence'). Obviously, a finding like this cannot be explained in terms of time. There is too, as we shall shortly see, the well established fact that different amounts of forgetting may occur over exactly the same time interval.

In summary, forgetting does not occur because of the passing of time. It occurs as the result of a number of factors which operate in time. The purpose of this chapter and of Chapter Five is to discuss the nature of these factors. This discussion will be concerned primarily with quantitative effects, with the way in which these factors affect the amount of forgetting. In Chapter Four we will see that these factors also influence the quality of forgetting, that they bring about changes in what is remembered by producing remarkable distortions of various sorts. In the meantime, we must introduce the causal factors themselves as they operate under rather artificial circumstances which, at first sight, may appear to have little to do with the rich and exciting phenomena of everyday remembering and forgetting.

It might, at this point, be as well to remind ourselves of what is meant by forgetting. Forgetting is the process, not directly observable in itself, which produces a decrement in remembering. The word forgetting is often used loosely in ordinary speech to refer simply to an inability to give some required piece of information. But this inability may not necessarily be the result of forgetting. It may result from our never having learned the information in the first place. If a long and difficult poem is read over casually and only once, it would be misleading to say, on a later occasion, that we have forgotten it – for the simple reason that we did not learn it to start off with. Ideally, forgetting occurs where something can be remembered at one time and cannot be so well remembered at some later time. It is concerned with a decrement in remembering, with the sort of situation where we cannot recall or recognize today what we could recall or recognize yesterday, or where we require more effort to relearn today what we could, under the same circumstances, have relearned yesterday more easily.

The major factors responsible for forgetting are five in number and fall into two broad categories. The first of these categories concerns what might be called maintenance processes. These are processes of a physiological kind which go on inside the person and have to do with the maintenance of health and life itself, serving the body's needs for growth and repair and recovery from fatigue and injury. Within this category, forgetting may be caused, first, by deterioration of the organic changes produced by learning and, second, by actual injury to or disease of the brain. Not a great deal is known about these two factors but, for the sake of completeness, they must be mentioned. The second broad category concerns not so much what transpires inside the person as what goes on between the person and his environment. This category might be called that of behavioural processes. It includes the three forgetting factors of retroactive interference, altered conditions during remembering, and repression. We will now consider, in turn, the contributions made to forgetting by each of the first four factors. The fifth factor, that of repression, will be considered in Chapter Five, not because it is of greater importance than the others but because the discussion of it provides a convenient starting point for the introduction of such topics as childhood memories, the remembering of pleasant and unpleasant experiences, and 'split personality'.

2 . DETERIORATION OF THE TRACE

The effects of learning persist by producing some more or less lasting change in the nervous system, by, to use the traditional phrase, laying down a neural trace in the brain. And the process responsible for the maintenance of this trace between the time of learning and that of remembering is, as has already been mentioned, that of retaining. It has also been mentioned that next to nothing is definitely known either about the trace itself or about the way in which it continues to exist. There is, nevertheless, the possibility that this trace (whatever its nature) deteriorates in time. When a muscle is frequently exercised, it draws nutriment from the blood stream and thereby maintains itself and even improves its condition. But when it is no longer in use, it cannot compete with the nutritional demands of other active muscles and organs; it has to give up some of its own substance and, in doing so, atrophies. It is conceivable that something of this sort may happen with the memory trace. If it remains inactive for some time, it may lose out in physiological competition with more active parts of the nervous system and, like the muscle, undergo some sort of atrophy or deterioration. This notion that the trace deteriorates as an indirect consequence of disuse is mere speculation. But it is plausible. And if there is no evidence to support it, neither is there any evidence to refute it. The trouble is that until physiologists are able to examine the working of the nervous system in greater detail, the case for or against forgetting in terms of deteriorated traces must remain, in the words of the Scottish legal verdict, not proven. So it would be understandable if we were less impressed by this possible explanation than by those which follow and are supported by definite empirical evidence. To suggest, in the present state of knowledge, an 'atrophy' explanation of forgetting would amount to little more than a confession of ignorance. But the possibility that an explanation of this sort may one day be substantiated should always be borne in mind.

3. CEREBRAL DYSFUNCTION

Professor R. S. Woodworth reports in his book *Experimental Psychology* the following personal experience.

A young man doing a little mountain climbing with friends falls on his head, being knocked unconscious for a moment and left in a dazed state for a couple of hours. We could not expect him to remember what happened during the dazed state, but the curious and psychologically significant fact is that his memory for the 15 minutes preceding the accident was blank and permanently so.

This blank period seems to occur regularly in accidents where a person is rendered unconscious by a blow on the head. It also occurs under the psychiatric treatment known as electro-convulsive therapy. Here, patients suffering from certain types of mental disorder benefit from having a brief electric current passed through their head. The shock produces unconsciousness and a short convulsion and, after the patient has recovered consciousness, he is unable to recall his experiences for the few minutes which preceded the shock. Thus, if a blow or electric shock throws the brain into a sudden subnormal condition, the effects of any immediately preceding learning are obliterated. This dramatic forgetting of events as a result of cerebral insult is known as retrograde amnesia (which literally means backward forgetting) and it suggests that the traces laid down by learning require some short time to consolidate, that if the physiological effects of learning are to persist they require time to 'settle down'. Experiments in which white rats served as subjects reveal that if a simple brightness discrimination is to be learned then the brain must be left in its normal state for some minutes. Shock given about an hour after learning leaves remembering (as measured by the relearning method) unimpaired. But rats receiving shock fifteen minutes or less after each trial show impaired remembering, and the sooner the shock is administered the greater is the impairment until, at about the twenty-second interval, there is complete and permanent forgetting. Much still remains to be discovered about the process of consolidation, but there can be little doubt as to its existence. Anything learned or experienced just before cerebral shock may be permanently forgotten because its traces were not sufficiently established.

The type of cerebral shock discussed above is a temporary and relatively mild affair which produces no lasting change in the condition of the brain as such. But there are people whose nervous systems are seriously damaged in consequence of a head injury, a disease, an infection, or a toxic condition. The behavioural changes produced by such damage are never of a simple nature, and one of the many problems being vigorously tackled by contemporary psychologists is the unravelling of the complex relationships between the nature of the injury sustained and the resulting changes in behaviour. As far as forgetting is concerned, it may be affected by brain dysfunction in one of two ways. There may be an impairment in the remembering of experiences which occurred prior to injury (retrograde amnesia) or there may be an impairment of subsequent learning and so, of course, of remembering (this is, rather inappropriately, termed auterograde amnesia). The injury may be such that the retention of previous learning effects is impossible and, here, forgetting is permanent and the learning can only be replaced, if at all, by a long process of re-education. Again, the injury may produce only temporary forgetting and ability to recall returns with the patient's recovery. The forgetting, whether permanent or temporary, may involve long stretches of previous experience and vast repertoires of the person's learned abilities. Where it is, for example, the use of language which is forgotten (aphasia), the defect may be predominantly on the expressive side, as when there is an inability to speak or write, or again, the defect may be mainly a receptive one, as when there is forgetting of how to understand spoken or written language. In short, the possible effects of brain dysfunction are almost limitless and it would be outside the scope of this book even to begin to consider them. One finding is, however, worth mentioning, since it relates to a fairly widespread fallacy regarding the recall ability of people in the early stages of senility. This finding is that forgetting which is due to organic deterioration is characteristically retrogressive.

In cases of diffuse brain disease, recent events are the first to be forgotten and, as the disease worsens, the forgetting involves events which lie further and further back in the person's life history. An excellent example of this retrogressive tendency was reported in 1950 by Professor O. L. Zangwill. The patient, a woman of 57, had a severe case of Korsakoff's psychosis. This is a condition of cerebral deterioration which is usually brought about by alcohol and of which a chief symptom is loss of remembering and learning ability. In this patient, the amnesia involved the fifteen years which preceded the onset of her illness. Earlier events were accurately recalled, but there was essentially no recall for experiences within the past fifteen years. She consistently underestimated her age by some ten or eleven years despite the fact that she knew the present year and also the date of her birth. But she was never fully convinced by any arithmetical demonstration of her true age. When asked to draw a woman dressed in the latest fashion, she drew a style of dress which had not been worn for some fifteen years. In all respects, she showed complete inability to remember events which had occurred during the fifteen years before her illness.

Now, retrogressive amnesia is also characteristic of the general cerebral incompetence often found in old age. As we grow old, there tends to be a gradual impairment of bodily and mental functions. In some persons, however, the cerebral deterioration outruns the general bodily dysfunction, and we have a condition known as 'senile dementia'. Here we have impairment of both learning and remembering. In the early stages, only the forgetting of recent events is noticeable. The old person complains that his memory is not what it was. The names of new acquaintances and of places recently visited are difficult to recall. He forgets appointments which fall outside the well-established routine. He repeats statements as though they had not been made just a short time before. He tells and retells to the same audience the same anecdotes with all the same tiresome circumstantial details. In short, he shows impaired ability to learn and retain new information and techniques and, in consequence, loses interest in the current developments with which he cannot keep abreast. This loss of learning ability might be regarded as a continuation, to the point of biological and social unadaptiveness, of that earlier decline which was noted in discussing memory span. As the condition worsens, forgetting spreads retrogressively. Friends who have died within the past few years are spoken of as though they were still alive and, in general, experiences which are more and more remote in time begin to be forgotten.

There is a common belief that, as recall of recent experiences wanes, earlier events are remembered with increasing clarity and accuracy. Certainly, the senile excel in recounting their early experiences and may recall them with great vividness, living, as it is said, in the past. But this need not reflect a genuine improvement in ability to recall these early events (in other words, reminiscence). It seems likely that there is no such improvement and that, far from improving, ability to recall early events most probably suffers impairment along with immediate recall. Because they were better learned initially and their recall has been more frequently rehearsed and because they present the individual in the favourable light of his prime, early experiences are more easily recalled than the much more recent ones. Therefore it is these experiences which the aged talk about in an attempt to compensate for their impaired condition and to keep from others (and from themselves) an awareness of their defect's severity. What was done in middle age may be better remembered at the age of 60 than at 80, but its recall represents, at the latter age, a greater part of the individual's equipment for coping with social situations. Unable to meet younger associates on an equal footing, the aged can often command respect and awe by their greater know-ledge of a bygone era – a knowledge which, it should be borne in mind, may be inaccurate although, in so far as it relates to unrecorded occurrences, its accuracy or otherwise is impossible to establish so long as the recall is self-consistent. And in many cases, there is very little consistency. One of the commonest techniques for overcoming the appearance of forgetfulness is that of rationalization, of fabricating a plausible sequence of events to replace that which cannot be recalled. In senile dementia such rationalizing occurs to an abnormal degree. It is possible to elicit every few minutes a different account of the way in which an acute patient came into hospital. In the space of an hour, he may say that he has been in hospital for a long time, that he walked into hospital yesterday, that he came by bus, and that he was driven to hospital in the car of a friend who may, in fact, have been dead for some years.

Regarding reminiscence in senility, the present evidence strongly suggests that it does not occur. If it does, it can only be to a minor extent due to the warming-up effect (see later) of the effort to recall early experiences.

4. RETROACTIVE INTERFERENCE

Retroactive interference refers to a decrement in remembering which is brought about by the interpolation of some particular activity between the time of the original learning and of the remembering. This effect is perhaps the most potent single factor in everyday forgetting. In order to demonstrate it clearly, an experimental procedure must be adopted which, at its simplest, can be schematized as follows.

	Time 1	Time 2	Time 3
Subject I	Learn A	Activity X	Remember A
Subject II	Learn A	Activity Y	Remember A

Subjects I and II represent two people, or more usually two groups of people, who are 'matched', that is, who are selected so as to be of the same age, sex, educational level, and, most important, of the same ability to learn the lesson being employed. This matching procedure involves a number of technical difficulties, but it can be achieved, if not always beforehand then certainly afterwards, when we need consider only those people who have learned the same amount in the same time. Subjects I and II both follow exactly the same procedure of learning some lesson (represented by A) and remembering it after a specific lapse of time. They differ, however, in the activity they pursue during the interval between Time 1 and Time 3. Activity X is usually a learning activity of some sort while Activity Y is ordinarily rather non-strenuous and may merely involve describing photographs or reading light literature. What we are eventually interested in is how much better Subject II remembers than does Subject I. And since the two subjects are matched and have been treated in exactly the same way, any difference n their remembering performances can be attributed to the difference between the interpolated activities X and Y.

The sort of results which emerge from the above type of experiment may be indicated by citing a study published in 1931 by J. A. McGeoch and W. T. McDonald. Their subjects were University students; their lesson A was a list of adjectives to be memorized; their activity x was the learning of a list of items which were more or less similar to the original adjectives; and their activity y simply involved reading jokes. The results were as follows.

Interpolated activity	Percent of adjectives recalled
Reading jokes	45
Learning 3-place numbers	37
Learning nonsense syllables	26
Learning adjectives unrelated to originals	22
Learning adjectives antonymous with originals	18
Learning adjectives synonymous with originals	12

These results leave us in no doubt as to the influence of interpolated activity on recall performance. They show, too, an increasing impairment in recall with increasing similarity between the interpolated activity and the original learning. Like findings occur in many other investigations and, from such studies, three significant relationships have emerged. First, the amount of interference is an increasing function of the similarity between the original and the interpolated activity. Second, the amount of interference is an increasing function of the amount of the interpolated activity, i.e. the more active we are in the interval, the more likely we are to forget. And third, the greater the degree of original learning, the less susceptible it is to interference, i.e. the better we learn the original task, the more likely we are to remember it despite interpolated activities.

The above results indicate that forgetting is not so much a matter of the fading away of old impressions as of their being 'crowded out' by new impressions. The learning of a new list of adjectives involves, to some extent, the unlearning of an old list and will also give rise to errors in remembering because of confusions between the new and the old. For this reason, the term 'retroactive interference' is apt to be misleading. The interference does not literally act back on the original learning because, of course, it is now over and done with. What is interfered with is, in the first place, the traces of past learning which may be altered by the new activity and, in the second place, the later remembering activity which may be impaired because of an inability to separate out the retained effects of the original from those of the interpolated lesson. That there are these two distinct ways in which interference can occur, that it can cause both unlearning and confusion during remembering, is something which has been established by experimental procedures which are too complex to describe here. The present point simply is that we must not be misled by the figurative term 'retroactive'; there is no question of the interference acting backwards in time. Incidentally, it follows from what has just been said that we might expect to find what could be called 'proactive interference'. And such indeed is the case. Not only does the second activity interfere with the first, but this first learning activity interferes with the second to make it more difficult to learn.

Having found that forgetting results from the interpolation of certain activities between learning and remembering, the interesting question arises: If there were no intervening activities whatever, would forgetting still occur ? What would happen if it were possible to place someone in a psychological vacuum between the time of learning and the time of remembering ? On the assumption that retroactive interference is the sole cause of forgetting, it would be predicted that no forgetting would occur. The Sleeping Beauty of the fairy tale would, on arousing from her century-long sleep, recall the events of a hundred years ago as vividly as if they were the events of yesterday. It is, unfortunately, impossible to put such a speculation to rigorous experimental test, for the simple reason that any living being is always active, if even to only a slight extent. However, we can go some way to answering the above question by finding out how rapidly forgetting occurs during sleep as contrasted with the rate of forgetting during workaday waking activity. Of the experiments which have investigated rate of forgetting under these two conditions, the earliest and most famous is that of two American psychologists, J. G. Jenkins and K. M. Dallenbach. Their investigation, reported in 1924, employed two senior University students as subjects. It took two months to perform and, during this time, each subject underwent over sixty different tests. Each test consisted of the learning and the later recall of a list of ten nonsense syllables. Under the waking condition, the list was memorized in the morning to a criterion of one errorless recitation, and the subject then went about his routine affairs to be called back, after a specified interval, for recall. Under the sleep condition, the list was learned at night after the subject was undressed and ready for bed: he then retired immediately to an improvised bedroom adjoining the experimental room and was awakened later for his recall. Under both conditions, four different time intervals were employed between learning and recalling, namely, 1 hour, 2 hours, 4 hours, and 8 hours.

The results of the Jenkins and Dallenbach experiment were almost identical for both subjects. After the different intervals, the average number of syllables recalled by both was as follows.

Number of hours since learning

	0	1	2	4	8
After sleeping	10	7·0	5·4	5·5	5·6
After waking	10	4·6	3·1	2·2	0·9

Results of the waking condition follow the usual course, namely, a sharp initial drop in recall followed by a progressively slower decline. In contrast, results for the sleeping condition show a slight initial drop followed, after the 2-hour interval, by no further forgetting. (The rise from 5·4 to 5·6 is too small to be accepted as indicating a genuine increase.) It is to be stressed that, at each interval other than zero, there is a real difference in the amount of forgetting which has occurred during sleep and during waking activity, that these differences are not due to any flaw in the conduct of the experiment and, moreover, that similar differences have been found by later investigators using both nonsense material and meaningful prose passages. There can be no doubt that the ordinary activities of daily life bring about a substantial degree of forgetting. In the words of Jenkins and Dallenbach, 'forgetting is not so much a matter of the decay of old impressions and associations as it is a matter of the interference, inhibition, or obliteration of the old by the new.'

It should be realized that, while the Jenkins and Dallenbach type of study demonstrates the presence of retroactive interference, it by no means proves that other forgetting processes are absent. It is possible, for example, that there may be some atrophy of the neural trace, since there is impairment of remembering even after sleep. However, this forgetting might also be due to retroactive interference, since the sleep condition is not such as to eliminate all activity between the time of learning and recall. Before sleep, the subject leaves the room, gets into bed, and may remain mentally active for as long as ten minutes: after sleep, he must waken again and make his way back to the experimental room: even during sleep, there may be such activity as dreaming. It can never be settled as to whether or not the interfering effects of these activities are sufficient to account for all the forgetting which occurs during sleep – not, at least, until the unlikely event of obtaining a control condition in which there would be no activity of any sort between the moment of reaching the learning criterion and the moment of beginning recall. Only if there were no forgetting during this psychological vacuum would it be possible to conclude that atrophy of the memory traces had been absent.

A practical question which arises out of the above type of investigation is: Would it be advantageous to study just before going to sleep rather than through the day ? The most likely answer seems to be that there would be no advantage one way or the other unless the material were to be remembered fairly soon after waking. If a lesson is learned at night, it will probably, in the first place, require more effort than in the relative freshness of morning. In the second place, retroactive interference will occur on the following day anyhow. Wherever night study did happen to be profitable it would be because little forgetting would occur during sleep and, on waking, the learner could return to the task refreshed and with renewed vigour.

We have spoken so far only about interference between two different tasks or activities. But important consequences also emerge from interference between the different parts of the same learning task. Thus, in learning a poem, the later parts will interfere with the traces of the earlier parts; and these earlier parts will, in their turn, make the learning of the later parts more difficult. The net result of this interference is that the most difficult part of any lesson will be the middle, since it is here that the greatest amount of both proactive and retro-active interference is concentrated. Again and again, experi-mental psychologists find that it is with the middle parts of a syllable list or poem or passage of prose that their subjects have the greatest difficulty. In everyday life, too, this is a common finding. We often recall the first few lines and the last few lines of a poem, the beginning and end of a lecture or novel, without being able to recall what comes in between. But, in addition to remembering the beginning or the end of some lesson, we also tend to remember parts of it which were 'striking'. This is also, to a great extent, the consequence of interference. The exceptional and unusual is 'noticed' and remembered better than what is monotonously similar. Everyone knows this, most of all those whose concern it is to sell commodities, be they toothpaste or political ideas. Advertisements need not be flamboyant to be effective, nor need people to become 'personalities'. But they must be distinct from their neighbours and stand out from among them. If we ask someone to memorize a list of, say, numbers in which a single syllable is inserted, we find that the isolated syllable will be learned quicker and remembered better than the average crowded number. This is because the similar items interfere with each other while the isolated item is relatively immune from such interference because of its lack of similarity to the items which precede and follow it. This same effect of interference is also apparent over long stretches of everyday living. The day on which lovers meet and wars break out is memorable. But not so the humdrum, uneventful periods of routine whose very lack of individuality ensures their being forgotten as unique events.

Qualitative Changes. This section has been devoted to discussing the importance of retroactive interference for for-getting. But this same interference process also plays a leading role in producing qualitative changes in what is remembered. That this is so can be readily demonstrated in the laboratory. We present our subjects with drawings or pictures or stories and then have them recall or recognize these at some later time: in the retention interval, we present some of the subjects with other material resembling the original and then find that their remembering of the original is distorted in consequence. There is, unfortunately, no space here to describe any of the ingenious and often amusing experiments which have been conducted along these lines, notably by such Cambridge psychologists as O. L. Zangwill and D. R. Davis. It must suffice to say that interpolated experiences may produce striking qualitative as well as quantitative changes in subsequent remembering. In the laboratory, these interpolated experiences are produced by presenting the subject with material somewhat resembling the original. But real-life interference may, in addition, result from the individual's own recalled or imagined experiences. Without assistance from outside, he provides his own interpolated and interfering experiences. In anticipation of Chapter Four, it might be said here that the mere fact of recalling an object, experience, or lesson may be sufficient to produce distortions. A specific example of this distorting effect of recalling may be given.

In 1955, the writer had, and made a note of, an interesting experience. This experience fell naturally into four parts and a shortened account of it is as follows.

(a) In the week beginning 23 October, I encountered in the Psychology Department of the University a male student of very conspicuously Scandinavian appearance. He was accompanied by a smallish, dark-haired companion and, as they seemed to be lost, I asked if I could help. The dark-haired student replied that his friend came from such-and-such a Scandinavian country and that he was looking for a certain lecturer. I then had the two men directed to this lecturer's room, and that was the end of the incident. I recall being very forcibly impressed by the Scandinavian man's nordic, Viking-like appearance – his fair hair, his blue eyes, and long bones. This nordic appearance was made all the more noticeable by the contrast between him and his companion. (b) About two hours later, I was leaving for lunch and met the Scandinavian student once more. I recognized him immediately and conversed with him as we walked out of the University together. Next day, I was speaking with the lecturer for whom he had been looking and discovered that his name was, we shall say, X (c) About two weeks later, without having seen X again, I found and recognized his name among those of some students whom I was to meet one day for tea. I wrote to X asking him to tea on 23 November. On several occasions, as well as at the time of writing to him, I recalled his appearance in connexion with a Scandinavian correspondence I was then conducting and thought of him as the 'perfect Viking', visualizing him at the helm of a long-ship crossing the North Sea in quest of adventure. On 18 November, I even gave this fanciful description of him to someone who was also coming to tea on the 23rd. (d) When X arrived on the 23rd, I did not recognize him and he had to introduce himself. It was not that I had forgotten what he looked like but that his appearance, as I recalled it, had become grossly distorted. Two things struck me. The first was that he was very different from my recollection of him. His hair was darker, his eyes less blue, his build less muscular, and he was wearing spectacles (as he always does). The second was that I had seen him twice in the interval since our first two encounters without recognizing him. On each occasion it had been at a meeting where there was no opportunity to speak but, each time, I had been struck by his Scandinavian looks and had speculated as to where his home might be and whether he might know any of my Scandinavian acquaintances.

The above sequence of events clearly illustrates that retro-active interference may stem from the individual's own recalling. It was not that the writer's original perceiving of X was at fault for if it had been, he would not have recognized X on the second encounter two hours later. It was that in subsequently recalling X, the writer had also recalled his personal stereotype of a Viking, and this latter recalled experience had moulded his subsequent recall of X to such an extent that X was not recognized when actually present. As recalled, X now resembled a 'perfect Viking' more than he did himself. Apart from this example, the writer has observed not a few instances of the interfering effect of recalling in his own activities. Buildings, objects, and people have been recalled in terms of those characteristics originally noticed as dominant, and these characteristics (of size, gloominess, colourfulness, etc.) have become sharpened and accentuated in being recalled until the building, object, or person – as recalled – is but a caricature which is much larger, more gloomy, or more colourful than the original ever was. On being seen again, the original is now almost or completely unrecognizable.

That recalling of an experience may interfere with the later recognition of it is not a phenomenon which is unique to the writer. It is, for example, well demonstrated in an experiment reported by Dr Eunice Belbin of Cambridge in 1950. She had thirty-two subjects in all (comprising ten naval ratings, eight 14-year-old children, and fourteen University students). At the beginning of the experiment, each subject was left sitting in a waiting room for two minutes. On the wall facing him was a large road-safety poster but the subject was given no instructions of any kind regarding it. As far as he was concerned, it had nothing to do with the experiment and he was simply waiting until the experimenter was ready for him. At the end of the two minutes, each subject was called into the experimenter's room and, after a short while, shown an identical poster and asked if this was the same as the poster in the waiting room. The ingenious turn in the experiment came in the interval between being in the waiting room and being asked to identify the poster. Half of the subjects (the recall group) were asked to describe as much as they could of the poster and their recalling was prompted by standardized questions. The remaining half of the subjects (the non-recall group) were occupied with an unrelated task during an equivalent period of time. Given the poster to identify, fourteen out of the sixteen non-recall subjects did so correctly without hesitation. But only four subjects in the recall group identified it as being the same. The difference between the two groups is significant and cannot be attributed to individual differences of any sort, especially in view of Dr Belbin's similar findings in other experiments of the same basic type. What happened was that the recall group constructed their recalling around the dominant features of the picture and thereby made these features more outstanding than in the original; they also invented one or two details, such as Belisha Beacons or an additional car, which they accepted as having been genuinely recalled. In short, the constructive character of their recalling (see Chapter Four) introduced distortions, omissions, and additions into the poster as recalled so that the poster, as later seen, appeared to be substantially different and was not recognized as being the same as the original. The non-recall group, on the other hand, were not hindered in their recognition by any distorted recall of the poster.

To conclude our discussion of retroactive interference, it is the decrement in remembering which is due to activities and experiences interpolated between original learning and later remembering. It is by far the most potent factor in bringing about forgetting and is often responsible not only for quantitative but also qualitative changes in what is remembered. The effects of interference increase with the amount of interpolated activity and with the similarity of this activity to the original; these effects show themselves most potent in the case of material which has not been well learned to start off with. At a practical level, this means that the original learning should be as thorough as possible and that if one period of study must be followed immediately by another, we should arrange to switch to that form of learning which is the least similar to the one in which we have just been engaged.

5. ALTERED CONDITIONS DURING REMEMBERING

The true story is told of the man who lived for several years in China and, by persistent application, managed to learn to speak Chinese. Then he left the Orient and came home for two years. At the end of this time, he had to return to China and, just before setting off, he discovered that he had all but completely forgotten his laboriously acquired Chinese. He naturally expected to have to learn much of it over again. Yet, on arrival, he was surprised to find that, in the Chinese setting once more, he could understand the language perfectly and speak it fairly fluently. He could remember in China what he could not remember at home. Here we have an example of temporary forgetting which is due to altered conditions in the environment. Learning takes place in a concrete setting; it involves a specific task which is carried out in a specific environment such as a particular school-room or town. And, although we may not be aware of it, this specific environment becomes a part of what is learned. In general it is true to say that if this environment is greatly altered during the time of attempted remembering then remembering will be impaired. We must all have experienced this phenomenon. We try to recollect what we did in some distant town and fail. Yet, on revisiting the original scene, 'it all comes back to us'. Many instances of this sort of thing have been reported in autobiographies, and psychologists have shown that it can be produced experimentally. When nonsense syllables are presented for learning against a coloured background, it requires more time to relearn them when presented against a different colour of ground than when the colour remains unchanged. Likewise, the introduction of a small audience produces some forgetting, as will be readily understood by anyone who has experienced 'stage fright'. When the classroom learning of school children is later examined in a different room, the amount recalled is smaller than when the exam takes place in the room where learning originally took place. Having a strange teacher in charge of the exam likewise impairs recall, and this impairment is even greater if both the room and the teacher are changed for the exam.

That recalling is facilitated by the presence of some part of the environment in which learning originally took place is recognized in the device of keeping mementoes or 'reminders'. Many people deliberately supply themselves with objects which will reintegrate, with greater or lesser success, the situations of which these objects were once a part. The photograph, the 'keepsake', the knot in the handkerchief all serve to reintegrate some past experience, to prompt our recalling of the reason for their being there. For the same reason, the medieval clergy built their *memento mori*. These gruesome effigies of decomposing bodies are still to be seen in many cathedrals, and their purpose was to remind their owners of the fact of their mortality. Thus, there are in history and in our everyday lives instances of the way in which we acknowledge the importance of reintegration for recalling.

Now, just as remembering is made easier by the presence of the appropriate physical environment, so too it is aided by an appropriate 'mental environment'. When we undertake to-day to perform some activity which we have previously learned, our initial attempts tend to be slow, irregular, and inexact. But as we persist in our attempt, we return to our former level of efficiency. When the typist returns to his machine, the musician to his instrument, the student to his studies, he starts 'cold' and requires some little time to 'pick up the thread' once more. This familiar phenomenon is known to psychologists as the 'warming-up effect' and it is as characteristic of remembering activity as of other skilled performances. If we are immersed in a chemistry problem and someone suddenly asks us about religious practices in Borneo, we may experience difficulty in recalling the answer until we have taken time to 'think ourselves into' the atmosphere of social anthropology.

A number of experiments have been performed which show that when people are plunged into a remembering task, they do not remember as well as they do if allowed to warm-up. In part of a study published in 1955 by the writer, a group of students was given exactly three minutes in which to write down all the surnames and Christian names which could be recalled beginning with the letter 'K'. The students were urged to make their list as long as possible and, on the average, recalled 11·5 such names. A second group of students was given the same task immediately after having performed a similar task in which they had to recall names beginning with a different letter (either 'N' or 'J'). These students did significantly better than the former group by recalling an average of 14·3 names beginning with 'K'. In recalling, say, N-names, these students warmed-up to this type of recall task and established a set which facilitated the subsequent performance of recalling K-names. It is to be noted that this specific set is rapidly lost for, if the two recall sessions are separated by twenty minutes or more, performance on the second shows no improvement over performance on the first. When he finishes his recall task, the student gives over his set in favour of others demanded by current activities and, on returning to recall once more, he cannot adopt the appropriate set straight away but requires a few minutes to warm-up again. We are familiar with this sort of thing in everyday life. The more we try to recall the details of some incident, the more we as it were steep ourselves in the incident, then the more vividly and completely are we likely to recall it.

The above discussion indicates that some part of everyday forgetting may be due to a lack of warming-up and that, if we can establish the appropriate set, our remembering will be enhanced. We may even remember more than we imagined at first to be possible. Direct evidence for this comes from studies in which people are asked to recall some poem or speech which they could once quote readily but which, in the meantime, they have almost completely forgotten. At first, they typically recall little except the general atmosphere of the original and perhaps one or two isolated phrases. A few more words may then be recalled and by the end of, say, twenty minutes the subject is prepared to claim that he can recall no more. But if he is asked to recall on the next day and, again, on the next for several days running, it is found that this confession of failure was premature. More and still more of the original is recalled. Sometimes the new words 'just happen' while attempted recall is in progress : sometimes they 'come out of the blue' at a time when the subject is relaxing and not thinking about the original at all : at other times some word which he happens to see or hear during his ordinary activities seems to 'stick', the subject finds himself thinking about it, and later makes the sudden discovery that it supplies a missing part of the original. In general, we find that with such repeated attempts at recall, the subject can reproduce at least twice as much of the original as he did at that earlier point where he claimed that he could not recall any more. Just why these repeated attempts should have the effect they do presents psychologists with a fascinating problem the solution of which is as yet but partly known. But this much is certain : attempted recall facilitates further recall and does so, in part, through the warming-up effect. Recall does not merely strengthen the recall of reported phrases and words, it also facilitates the recall of hitherto unreported parts of the original. Thus, with an adequate degree of warming-up, we can recall much more than we at first imagined possible.

In summary of this section, it may be said that forgetting may occur because certain conditions are not present at the time of attempting to remember. These conditions are environmental on the one hand and attitudinal on the other. And when these appropriate conditions are reinstated, remembering is enhanced.

Before leaving this chapter, one small point should be made explicit, although it ought already to have become apparent. There is no one cause of forgetting. We have considered several of the major factors in forgetting and it is clear that all of them may operate at one and the same time. In the laboratory and in his writings, the psychologist considers examples of forgetting in which one factor operates in isolation from the others. But in most real life situations, it is by no means obvious that this particular factor is at work rather than that, and not enough is known about the circumstances to make a definite judgement one way or the other. To ask the reason for any specific occurrence of forgetting is, very often, to ask for the impossible. All that can be done is to give a number of possible reasons, any or all of which may be valid for this particular instance.

CHAPTER FOUR

RECALLING STORIES AND EVENTS

1. THE EFFECT OF INTERPRETING

THE chief concern of the two preceding chapters has been with quantitative aspects of memory, with how much is remembered and how much is forgotten. But if someone witnesses a street accident and is later required to give evidence in a law court, it is almost certain that his recall will be distorted as well as incomplete. Further, his account of the incident may differ in quite fundamental respects from that of another witness. Obviously, his performance is not merely a question of recalling more or less of the original: there are also qualitative changes to be considered. The purpose of this chapter is to consider the nature of these qualitative changes as they manifest themselves in verbal recall, as they occur when people describe their past experiences in words.

The kinds of changes which are likely to occur are illustrated in the results of an experiment reported by two Cambridge psychologists, J. Blackburn and E. J. Lindgren. Without the knowledge of the people present, they made a recording of the discussion which followed a meeting of the Cambridge Psychological Society. Two weeks later, they wrote to all those who had attended and asked them to write down all they could recall about this discussion. When the reports were received, they were checked against the recorded version and it was found that the average number of specific points recalled by any individual was only 8·4 per cent of the total recorded. However, the really remarkable thing about these recalled points was that, on the average, no less than 42 per cent of them were substantially incorrect. A large variety of errors and confusions appeared. Happenings were reported which had never taken place at all or which had taken place on some other occasion and were wrongly recalled as having occurred at this particular discussion. Thus, a person might report a colleague as making a remark which he knew this colleague habitually made but which he did not happen to make on this particular occasion, e.g. the formal thanking of the speaker by the chairman of the meeting. There were also elaborations, as when some casual remark was expanded into a fairly lengthy contribution to the discussion or when a point was reported as having been made explicitly whereas it had only been hinted at. In short, what was recalled was not only fragmentary but also distorted and much was recalled which, in fact, had never happened.

Why should there be this inaccuracy in recall? What kinds of inaccuracy are to be expected? These are the questions raised by observations such as those above. The first psychologist to tackle these questions in a systematic way was Professor (now Sir) Frederic Bartlett of Cambridge. In a series of ingenious experiments, he presented people with complex pictures and stories and examined the distortions contained in later recall. He published his findings in 1932 in a book entitled *Remembering*. No brief summary could do justice to the rich observations and sensitive insights contained in this classic of psychological literature. The book's major import, however, is this: both learning and remembering are profoundly influenced by the process of interpreting, by what Bartlett calls 'rationalizing' or the 'effort after meaning'. This section is devoted to a discussion of what is meant by interpretation. In the following section, a fairly detailed report will be given of some experimental findings which illustrate its effect.

We human beings universally and spontaneously try to understand, to make sense of any situation which presents itself. And the way in which we do this is to relate the new situation to those situations which we have encountered in the past. A child, on seeing his first squirrel, might call it a 'funny bunny'. He fits the new experience into the scheme of things – as he understands it – by describing this creature as a rabbit with a difference. He interprets his new experience in terms of his past experiences. In the course of his lifetime, he has acquired a body of knowledge and expectations about the sorts of objects and events which occur in the world around him and he tries to fit the new and unfamiliar into this already familiar pattern. If it fits, then it makes sense for him, it has meaning, he knows 'where he is' and what to do about it. If it does not fit, it remains strange and perplexing in the way that modern art does to the unsophisticated observer who complains of its lack of meaning. The various bodies of knowledge which we have all built up on the basis of past experience have been called, by Bartlett, *schemata* (the singular is *schema*): the process of interpreting the unfamiliar, of fitting it into this or that schema, has been called *assimilation*.

It is important to realize that these schemata are not rigid affairs. They are ongoing, cumulative processes. They are active organizations of past experience which not only accommodate but also adapt themselves to new experiences. The most obvious analogy is, perhaps, that of a filing cabinet where correspondence can be filed under various heads according to subject matter. In order to 'make sense', each letter must be filed under one or other heading. But as more and more letters come in, covering an increasing range and diversity of topics, it is constantly necessary to rearrange the files, to subdivide them, reclassify them, and cross-index them. Each office builds up its own filing arrangement to suit its own particular type of business and its files determine how incoming correspondence will be dealt with. So too, we, as individuals, build up our schemata in accordance with our social and educational background and our own interests and needs. And these schemata affect the way in which we interpret the happenings around us. That this is so is illustrated by the old anecdote concerning the botanist, the geologist, and the artist who went together for a country walk. They passed along the same road at the same time, yet they saw different things. The botanist saw the plants which grew by the roadside. The geologist saw the rock formations. The artist saw the interplay of colour and light and shade. The three men might almost have been traversing different roads, for there were distinct differences in the ways they actually perceived or experienced their surroundings. At the experimental level, too, there has been abundant evidence for the fact that we interpret our present experiences in accordance with our own interests, attitudes, hopes and expectations. It has been found, for example, that, as compared with people who regard

Negroes in a favourable or unprejudiced light, those with anti-Negro attitudes find difficulty in distinguishing one Negro from another. They see a Negro in somewhat the same way as the average person sees a sheep, not as an individual with unique characteristics but merely as a member of an undifferentiated class. Again, there is the fact that if we show a blurred and indistinct picture to a hungry man, he is more likely to see it as representing food or some object related to food than is a man who is not hungry. These examples all illustrate the great, but perhaps not immediately apparent, truth that we each experience the world about us in our own way. To misquote the words of the poet, it is not only beauty which lies in the eye of the beholder. The important point, as far as memory is concerned, is simply this: that we interpret the events around us in accordance with our own accumulated past experiences and present needs. We relate the unfamiliar to the familiar, assimilate it to our schemata, infuse it with personal meaning. And, for the most part, this effort after meaning is not deliberate but immediate and accomplished without our being aware of it.

This subtle and often unconscious process of interpretation exerts a dual effect on our recall of stories and events. In the first place, it affects our original perception of the situation. The same drama may be played out before two spectators each of whom will, as is popularly and so rightly said, put his own construction on it. Secondly, it affects our recall of the event. Much that is accepted as recall is, in actuality, reconstruction. Our account of an event is usually not so much an accurate reproduction as an elaboration of fragmentary recollections into a coherent caricature of the original. In the light of our general expectations about events, we construct, out of a few elements, an account of what was likely to have occurred. We reconstruct our own past experiences in much the same way as a zoologist might reconstruct, out of a few fossilized remains, the appearance of some long extinct animal. For example, a colleague of the writer's once reported having seen a certain Mrs X at a party the week before. He even added that she was wearing the same old dress in which she invariably attired herself for such occasions. But it was later discovered that

Mrs X had not attended the party but had, in fact, been some miles away visiting friends. Taxed with this information, the colleague realized that he could not have seen Mrs X but that he had recalled seeing her husband and 'naturally assumed' that she too had been there since they always attended such gatherings together. In all sincerity, he had inferred rather

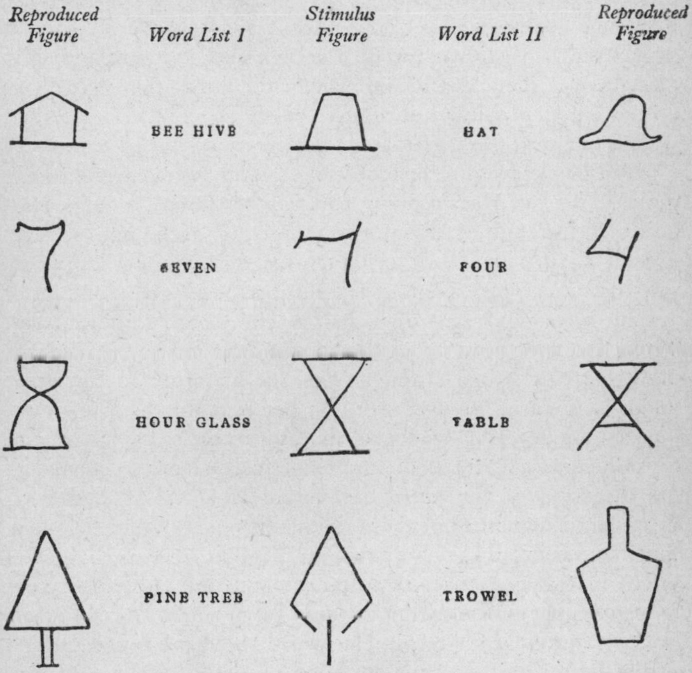

Reproduced Figure	Word List I	Stimulus Figure	Word List II	Reproduced Figure
	BEE HIVE		HAT	
	SEVEN		FOUR	
	HOUR GLASS		TABLE	
	PINE TREE		TROWEL	

Fig. 2

than reproduced the events of that evening and his inference was all the more evident because it happened to be wrong. In everyday life, we often, as it were, fit together recalled bits and pieces in a patchy mosaic and fill out the gaps by inference. But the constructive nature of our recall tends to pass unnoticed either because the construction is correct or because we have no reason or opportunity to check up on the true facts. It is under the more carefully controlled conditions of the laboratory that we come to appreciate the full extent to which recalling is pervaded by inference and imagination.

As an example of the overall effect which interpretation has on recall, we may cite an experiment which was conducted in 1932 by the American psychologist Leonard Carmichael along with two other colleagues. The material used was a list of twelve more or less ambiguous line drawings. Four of these drawings are shown in Fig. 2. Adult subjects were told that they would be shown these drawings and that, immediately afterwards, they would be asked to draw the figures as accurately as possible but in any order. The figures were then shown one at a time. However, before each, the experimenter said: 'The next figure resembles . . .' and gave a name to the figure. The purpose in doing this was to direct, through suggestion, the subject's interpretation of each figure. The ingenious turn in the experiment was that, while all subjects saw the same figures, half of the subjects were given one set of verbal labels and the other half a completely different set. Thus, the first drawing in Fig. 2 was labelled a 'beehive' for one group of subjects and a 'hat' for another. In the great majority of cases (an average of 87 per cent for the four drawings shown here), it was found that, when the subjects came to reproduce any figure, their drawings were clearly distorted in the direction of the particular verbal label which had been supplied. The nature of these distortions is apparent from the specimen reproductions shown in Fig. 2. The verbal label acted, in the first place, by predisposing the subject to perceive, say, the first drawing as resembling a hat. In the second place, it moulded his recall. He would recall the rough outline of the figure and perhaps some of its detail. He would also recall that it crudely represented a hat and his final drawing would be biased accordingly.

2. 'THE WAR OF THE GHOSTS'

It has already been mentioned that the most comprehensive attempt to study the remembering of complex material was that of Bartlett. He would present an adult with a story, or an argumentative prose passage, or a picture, and have him recall it some days, weeks, or even years afterwards. In his Method of Repeated Reproduction, he asked the same individual to recall the same event again and again at intervals. If the reproductions were given frequently and at short intervals, he found that they rapidly became fixed in form while, if long intervals elapsed between successive reproductions, the process of gradual transformation continued almost indefinitely. In his Method of Serial Reproduction, he adopted a procedure which duplicated, to some extent, the conditions under which rumours spread from one person to another and legends are handed down from one generation to the next. He had one person reproduce the original; he then handed this reproduction to a second person; this second person's reproduction was presented to a third, and so on. Both of these methods – of repeated and serial reproduction – yielded results which are of interest not only to the study of memory but also to the study of rumour and folk-lore. Subsequent investigations, conducted mainly in Cambridge, have extended and refined Bartlett's conclusions. But Bartlett's book still remains the most comprehensive account of this type of psychological research. Results cannot be given in detail here, but what can be done is to take one of the pieces of material used by Bartlett and give some indication of the qualitative changes which occur when people try to reproduce it. The material is a story adapted by Bartlett from the translation of a North American folk-tale and is entitled 'The War of the Ghosts'. The story is of interest since, coming from another culture, it presents difficulties to British people because of the strange conventions and beliefs which it reflects, its apparently disconnected narrative, and the purely decorative detail which it contains. First, some results will be presented which were obtained by the writer. A discussion will then be given of the characteristic changes which occur with regard to this particular story.

The writer explained to a group of students that a story would be heard and that it was to be repeated as accurately as possible by one of them. It was also explained that the first retelling of the story would be heard by a second student who had not heard the original. This second student would then reproduce the story for a third student who would be hearing it for the first time. The third student would retell the story to a fourth, and so on. Seven students were then asked to volunteer as subjects and six of them left the room. The remaining student listened carefully to the story and the second student was called in to hear the first student recount the story as accurately as he could. This procedure was repeated with the remaining five subjects, the last simply telling the story to the group. The original story and each re-telling of it was recorded on a tape machine so that the entire series of reproductions could be played back to the assembled class. A specimen series of reproductions, written down verbatim from the recording, is given below. It should be pointed out that this specimen is not selected because of being unusually dramatic. The writer has used this experiment repeatedly as a classroom demonstration and the example to be given is typical of his collection of records.

Original Story: The title of this story is 'The War of the Ghosts'. One night two young men from Egulac went down to the river to hunt seals, and while they were there it became foggy and calm. Then they heard war-cries, and they thought: 'Maybe this is a war-party.' They escaped to the shore, and hid behind a log. Now canoes came up, and they heard the noise of paddles, and saw one canoe coming up to them. There were five men in the canoe, and they said: 'What do you think ? We wish to take you along. We are going up the river to make war on the people.' One of the young men said: 'I have no arrows.' 'Arrows are in the canoe', they said. 'I will not go along. I might be killed. My relatives do not know where I have gone. But you', he said, turning to the other, 'may go with them.' So one of the young men went, but the other returned home. And the warriors went on up the river to a town on the other side of Kalama. The people came down to the water, and they began to fight, and many were killed. But presently the young man heard one of the warriors say: 'Quick, let us go home: that Indian has been hit.' Now he thought: 'Oh, they are ghosts.' He did not feel sick, but they said he had been shot. So the canoes went back to Egulac, and the young man went ashore to his house, and made a fire. And he told everybody and said: 'Behold I accompanied the ghosts, and we went to fight. Many of our fellows were killed, and many of those who attacked us were killed. They said I was hit, and I did not feel sick.' He told it all, and then he became quiet. When the sun rose he fell down. Something black came out of his mouth. His face became contorted. The people jumped up and cried. He was dead.

First Reproduction: The title of this story is 'The War of the Ghosts'. Two young men went out to hunt seals. It was foggy. They heard war-cries and hid behind a log. Then they heard the splash of paddles and a canoe came up in which there were five young men. 'Come with us' they said 'we are going to make war on the people up the river.' One of the young men went with them (long pause) and took part in the battle which followed. He saw one of the Indians being killed and someone shouted: 'He is killed, let us go home now.' He felt sick and someone told him that he had been hit. They left and returned to the village. (Long pause.) He did not feel well the next morning. Something black came out of his mouth and he was dead.

Second Reproduction: The title of this story is 'The War of the Ghosts'. The interest of the story takes place in a foggy situation with a group of people in a small boat. The idea of the story is a seal hunt. There are five men who prepare to go upon this seal hunt and they select one of their number to accompany them to a battle. This battle occurs between some Indians and, in the course of the battle, evidently someone is killed and evidently it is this one individual who has been selected to accompany this group. Then someone shouts: 'Let's go home. He's been hit – or something's been done to him.' So they find themselves back in the original situation – back where they were. And this selected individual finds himself rather ill. And in the course of a day or so, this illness seems to become worse. And eventually something black comes out of his mouth and he's dead.

Third Reproduction: On a foggy day, five men go out on a seal hunt. They select one of the men – no – while they're out in the seal boat, a battle breaks out somewhere or other and they select one of the five to fight in this battle. So he is hit in the battle and he dies after a day or so, after the illness has worsened. And the others decide to – er – er – go back to the seal hunt. One of them has been hit for a second time in the battle and something black comes out of his mouth and he dies.

Fourth Reproduction: On a foggy day, five men go out in a boat on a seal hunt. While they're there, a battle breaks out and one of the men is sent to fight. He gets wounded and later dies. The other four men decide to continue on the seal hunt. One of these has been wounded and becomes sick. He too, later, dies, something black coming out of his mouth.

Fifth Reproduction: Five men set out in a boat on a seal hunt. While they were there, a battle breaks out. One of the men is killed in the battle. The other four continue on the hunt but one of them has been wounded and he becomes worse and dies with something black coming out of his mouth.

Sixth Reproduction: Well, five men were out on a seal hunt. One dies. That leaves four. The four go on their way. They start scrapping with each other and soon one of them is killed and something black comes out of his mouth.

Seventh Reproduction: Five men go on a seal hunt. One of them dies. That leaves four of them. One of them goes away. The other three start scrapping. One of *them* dies and something black comes out of his mouth.

Two points strike us at once regarding the above series. First, the story is much shortened. This is really no more than is to be expected since few adults could, at a single hearing, memorize the original word for word. Much is necessarily omitted. Notice that, as the tale becomes shorter, each successive version omits progressively less. Had the series been continued, we would have found it settling down to a relatively fixed form – a form which is sufficiently terse and conventional to be grasped and reproduced with literal accuracy. Second, despite omissions, the story becomes more coherent. There is no question of isolated and unrelated recall of bits of the original. The story, no matter how distorted it becomes, remains a story to the end. This is because the subjects interpret the story as a whole, both in listening to it and in retelling it.

With the Method of Serial Reproduction, changes take place which are more dramatic than those found in the Method of Repeated Reproduction where having experienced the original acts as a certain restraint to improvisation. This is especially the case under the conditions of the present experiment where the subject is reproducing the story orally in front of an audience and so under a degree of mild stress. If he were writing out the story with time at his disposal, he would check and re-check his statements, correct his ambiguous expressions, and produce a narrative which is as explicit and orderly as he can make it. Here, he cannot do this. He may know what he wants to say but, because of nervousness or inarticulateness, he may not express himself as clearly as he would like. And some imperfection in the wording, some alteration in the order of events, some omission which, at the time, seems trivial may be misinterpreted by his hearer and so prepare the way for a succession of further and more dramatic changes. Now, it might be argued that all this additional opportunity for mis-understanding would rob the above demonstration of its value. There are, however, two good reasons why this is not so. First, it often happens in everyday life that gossip, rumours, and so on are passed round by word of mouth under conditions where fluster and distraction are present. Just con-sider the news which is exchanged over coffee cups! Second, even where conditions are most favourable to quiet and reflective recall, the same kinds of distortion appear as are reported above – especially if we try to recall any event which happened a long time ago. It is found that long-distance recall involves both the presence of one or two isolated details and also the presence of the general setting, expressed mainly through the subject's emotional attitude to the original event. Sometimes, only the details are present: a name, a phrase, a perfume, a sound – and nothing else. Sometimes, only the general atmosphere is present: we may recall only the un-pleasantness, the eeriness, or the exhilaration of the situation. But detail and 'tone' may both be present. And it is when this happens that recall is most conspicuously inferential and con-structive in character. What the above demonstration does is to elicit, over a short time interval and in an exaggerated way, exactly those changes which have been found by Bartlett and others to occur, over a longer time interval, in real life.

Further examples of distortion can be seen in the five addi-tional records given at the end of this section. These were obtained from five different groups of students by a procedure identical with that outlined above and each record is the seventh version of an independent reproduction series. The reader should compare these versions with the original. In this way, he will probably learn more about the qualitative changes involved in remembering complex events than he could by reading any brief description of them. It may, however, be helpful to consider, in very general terms, the conclusions pointed to by these experiments with 'The War of the Ghosts'.

The major conclusion is that interpreting plays a major, and usually unrecognized, role in the remembering of stories and events. The event, as perceived and as recalled, has to be connected, certainly as a whole and, if possible, as regards its details also, with something which is already familiar. A story which is foreign to the subject's mode of thinking is not recalled accurately either in general theme or in detail. Events drop out of the account unless they can be fitted into a familiar framework either naturally or in that specially incongruous way which provides an unexpected dramatic or comic turn of events. All this is evident in 'The War of the Ghosts'. At one reading or hearing, British subjects fail to grasp the true nature of the theme. The wound becomes an affair of the flesh rather than of the spirit; the initial appearance of the warriors remains unexplained; and the ghosts either drop out of the story altogether, or remain in a rather detached context, or are brought in at the end as a comic or dramatic climax. The interpretation which any one person puts on the story may be unusual and its rationale not immediately apparent. Such individualistic interpretations often mark distinct turning-points in a series of reproductions but, as we would expect, they rarely survive in their original form. In being passed on from subject to subject, the story becomes, in a word, conventional. It retains only those characteristics which can be readily assimilated to that background of past experience which all the members of the chain share in common. The story is shorn of its individualizing features, the descriptive passages lose most of what peculiarities of style and content they possess, and the original phrasing is replaced by current, commonplace *clichés*. When descriptive and argumentative passages are used as material, conventionalization and a bias towards the concrete are also found. Illustrative examples survive the general moral which they point; every argument or piece of reasoning is quickly dropped and replaced by a bald expression of fact or of conventional opinion.

An instructive illustration is reported by Bartlett of the way in which the person's cultural background determines which elements of an experience will be dominant. He used 'The War of the Ghosts' in experiments which were conducted both during and after the 1914–18 war. During the war, the first excuse given by the young men for not joining the war-party ('we have no arrows') was rarely retained by his men subjects, whereas the second excuse (referring to relatives) persisted in almost all cases. At this time, these men had either seen war service or were likely to do so soon. Thus, it seems probable that this part of the story reminded them of their own situation. Indeed, some subjects admitted that it did. The reference to relatives was personally relevant. In experiments conducted after the war, it was found that this second excuse, like the first one, tended to drop out since it played a small part in the central theme of the story. Once social conditions had removed the anxious preoccupation with the possible effects of war service on relatives, there was a reduced tendency for the second excuse to be outstanding.

An element of the story which is conspicuously difficult for British subjects to assimilate is the 'sympathetic weather'. In the original, the coming of the warriors is heralded by fog and calm just as, in many plays and novels, a storm blows up at the moment of tragedy or peaceful skies accompany a happy ending. This sympathetic weather is often reacted to as establishing an eerie mood, yet it is rarely reproduced as such. The title of the story, too, is commonly omitted although it is clearly enough stated in the original presentation. It seems as though both the title and the sympathetic weather belong to a class of features which are effective in setting up a vague expectation of what is to follow but which are not, in themselves, outstanding details. Like the unusual literary style of the original, the impression they make is general rather than specific. They contribute to the subject's interpretation of the story without being remembered in detail.

The last of the common omissions are definite numbers and proper names. These usually disappear altogether and, if they do not, they are transformed or transposed. For example, 'Kalama' may be transformed into 'Colombo' and – as in the above record – the number five may persist but be transposed from its original context to another part of the story. Omission goes, of course, hand in hand with an emphasizing of what is retained. And, in certain instances, this emphasis is pointed up by elaboration. The elaboration usually involves the adding of detail as where the young man's reference to his relatives is expanded and made more concrete in the statement that 'he had a wife and family to look after'. Elaboration may, however, involve the invention of whole new episodes when the story is of the cumulative, repetitive, house-that-Jack-built variety. A tendency towards this cumulative elaboration seems to be showing itself in the later versions of the series recorded above.

This section may now be concluded by quoting a number of versions of 'The War of the Ghosts' which occurred, in different groups of adult British subjects, at the end of a reproduction series.

Seventh Reproduction of Group A: Well, this is a story about a battle between some ghosts. Five chaps went to hunt for seals. They arrived on a rocky coast and discovered another five chaps hiding behind a rock. They asked them if they would join in the hunt and one of them refused because he had no arrows. The other four went off to fight in a battle. It was a great battle and everyone was killed. Well, when the chaps came back, the one they had left behind was dead also.

Seventh Reproduction of Group B: This is a story about warriors and ghosts. The warriors went down to a lake where they met some men in a boat. One of the warriors got an arrow in his back. He felt no pain but his face was distorted. So he went back to bed where he felt better.

Seventh Reproduction of Group C: This is the story of two men who went fishing for seals. The story took place in Canada or India or some place like that. When they were out fishing, they saw five men in the distance. They wanted to fight with them and so they had a battle. During the battle, two of the men were killed. And they went back and told their parents.

Seventh Reproduction of Group D: There were two men in a canoe. They paddled along and came to a village. They both got out. They went to the village. They went back to the canoe and got into it. Then something black came out of the mouth of one of them and he fell dead. And then the other one fell dead too.

Seventh Reproduction of Group E: This story concerns three young men in a place called Igula. And they decided to have a trip up country and they went in a canoe taking bows and arrows with them. They went up so far, up to a part of the country called Colombo. But they found nothing at all and so they came back again. After a few days, one of the men became ill and yet none of them had been hurt in any way during the trip.

3. GIVING TESTIMONY

In practical life, we may be called upon to give an account to others of some incident which we have witnessed. We are present at the scene of a crime and, some time later, we are asked in a law court to give a description of what happened and answer questions about it. Even outside the field of jurisprudence, we often require, in the give and take of social life, to recount our experiences to our friends and satisfy their curiosities about them. The question arises, especially in the light of what was said above: How adequate is our account? Alfred Binet, the famous French psychologist, tackled this question experimentally as long ago as 1900 and, in the early years of the century, many others followed his lead in conducting investigations into testimony. In outline, the method of investigation is simple. The subject is, say, shown a picture, the picture is then removed and, after a lapse of time, he is asked to describe it. His description can be elicited by merely asking him to tell or to write down as much as he can recall. He can simply be asked for a 'report', that is, a free account. On the other hand, he can be asked questions about the details of the picture. This interrogation can be restricted to such aspects as have not been mentioned by the witness in his report: or it can be conducted by preparing a list of questions which cover exhaustively all the contents of the original and are posed to all witnesses in the same order and in the same manner. The answers to these questions must be considered separately from statements which are made spontaneously and, in contrast to the report, they are said to constitute a 'deposition'.

In interrogating a witness, much has been found to depend on the form of the questions asked, particularly if they are of the type known as 'leading' or 'suggestive'. Since most of us are not ordinarily aware of the many subtly different forms which the 'same' question can take, it will probably be instructive to characterize briefly six of the main forms which can be distinguished. A 'determinative' question is the least suggestive of all and is simply introduced by a pronoun or interrogative adverb, e.g. 'What colour was the dog?' A 'completely disjunctive' question forces the witness to choose between two specified alternatives, e.g. 'Was there a dog in the picture?' can only be answered by a 'yes' or a 'no'. An 'incompletely disjunctive' question offers a choice between two alternatives but does not completely preclude a third possibility, e.g. 'Was the dog white or black?' For many witnesses, and especially for children, this form of question is, in practice, completely disjunctive, since a certain independence is required in the choice of the third possibility, for example, that the dog was neither white nor black but was brown. An 'expectative' question is one which arouses a moderately strong suggestion of the answer by framing the question negatively, e.g. 'Was there not a dog in the picture?' An 'implicative' question is one which implies the presence of something which was not actually present in the original, e.g. 'What colour was the cat?' in reference to a picture which did not contain a cat. Lastly, a 'consecutive' question is any form of question used to augment a suggestion which has been developed by a previous question. In addition to these six forms of question, it is found that a question is more suggestive if it asks whether certain things happened or were present rather than whether the witness saw or heard them. Furthermore, any leading question increases in suggestiveness if it comes from the lips of someone who, to the witness, appears authoritative and (as we say with a revealing double use of the word) imposing.

Once the report or deposition has been obtained, it can be analysed under three main heads. First, there is the range, that is, the number of items mentioned. Second, there is the accuracy of each item as compared with the original. Third, there is the degree of assurance with which an item is given: this varies all the way from the total uncertainty reflected in 'I don't know' to the certainty which is so complete that the witness is willing to take an oath that his statement is correct.

Many experiments of the above sort have been performed. As regards the original experience, the favourite has been the showing of a picture. This is usually detailed and depicts, say, a harvest or a fishing scene in which there are a number of people and a variety of objects and activities. But random collections of objects have also been used, and so too have more real-life events. Carefully rehearsed little 'dramas' have been performed in a natural context and in an apparently spontaneous way. Or again, as in the experiment of Blackburn and Lindgren, the event may be one which, although recorded, is genuinely unrehearsed. It might be expected that these testimony experiments would yield rich observations on many facets of memory. And such indeed is the case. A few of the major findings may now be highlighted. Incidentally, it is to be emphasized that these findings are obtained from people who are performing to the best of their ability. We can never be absolutely certain that deliberate falsification is absent from any account, but the experiments are conducted in such a way that there is little reason to mistrust the subjects' sincerity. Lying is, of course, an interesting social phenomenon but it is not one which is relevant in the context of a book on memory.

The completely accurate testimony is rare. The errorless account is an exception even when given by competent people under favourable conditions. Thus, one German investigator collected a total of 240 testimonies and found only five errorless reports and one errorless deposition. These errorless accounts are commonly given by witnesses who are extremely cautious and make only those few statements of which they are absolutely certain. It is also found that a detail may be in error even although it is given by the majority of witnesses. The testimony of the majority may be as inaccurate as that of the minority. Especially is this so with short time intervals between events: these are usually overestimated. It also tends to happen with the sequence of events, with the exact time of day at which they took place, with the relative spatial positions of people or objects in a scene, and with definite numbers of objects. These details are particularly liable to errors of interpretation and tend to be recalled in accordance with what would normally be expected rather than in accordance with what was, in fact, the case. A good example of this distorting effect of interpretation is given by the German psychologist, William Stern. During a lecture, a strange man walked into the room, asked permission to look at a book on one of the shelves there, spent a short time reading in the room, and then went away taking the book with him. The incident had, of course, been carefully rehearsed and one important feature of it was the taking away of the book, since the removal of any book from that room was strictly against the regulations. During the incident, the lecture continued and the students paid no particular attention to the stranger or to what he was doing. A week later, these students were asked to report on the incident and then answer a comprehensive list of questions concerning it. They might reasonably have declined to commit themselves on the grounds that they had paid very little attention at the time. However, they avoided this cautious procedure and made numerous statements about the man's appearance and actions. Many of these were, of course, incorrect. In the interrogation, the crucial question was: 'What happened to the book he was reading?' A few students answered this correctly and a few abstained from answering, but the majority declared unhesitatingly and in all sincerity that the man returned the book to its shelf.

The effect of the interrogation is to elicit more statements than appear in the report but also to reduce the overall accuracy of testimony. In quite a number of investigations, for example, it is found that the proportion of inaccurate items (contained in all the items given in testimony) is something like a tenth for report and a quarter for deposition. It is understandable why this should be so. In giving a report, the witness is free to describe only those circumstances which he can recall vividly and with a certain assurance. But as soon as he is interrogated, he may have to deal with features of the original which he can recall but vaguely, if at all. To be sure, it is always possible for him to say: 'I don't know.' But, in not a few cases, the witness is unprepared to confess his ignorance. It is as though the very fact of being questioned constrains him to feel that he must give an answer – and that he is capable of giving it. So, what he can recollect but dimly and inaccurately is constructed into a definite reply to the question posed. It may be that this reply is not formulated with full conviction but, rather, is given to satisfy the demands of an insistent interrogator. But once the reply has actually been given, there is a tendency for the witness to leave doubts behind and accept it as the outcome of genuine recall, especially if the interrogator seems to be satisfied with the answer and proceeds to ask further 'consecutive' questions. Now, if merely being questioned is likely to lead to false testimony, how much more must this be so when the questions are put in suggestive form. This is especially true when the witness is a child. It is found that children are inferior to adults in both the range and accuracy of their testimony, that is, they give fewer items and what they do give is more likely to be inaccurate. In part, this is due to their poorer ability to·observe, to understand, and to use language – all natural consequences of their more limited past experience. But, in part, it is due to their greater suggestibility. They are particularly likely to answer leading questions in accordance with the suggestion they carry. Thus, William Stern has estimated that 7-year-old children are misled by some 50 per cent of leading questions as contrasted with 18-year-olds who are misled by only some 20 per cent of such questions.

The assurance with which testimony is given is found to be no absolute guarantee of accuracy. Less error is found in sworn testimony than in unsworn, but inaccuracies still remain, especially if there has been a considerable lapse of time since the original experience. This is illustrated by figures which the writer has recalculated from data published by Karl Dallenbach, an American psychologist, in 1913. These figures are given below. Dallenbach allowed fifteen men students to scrutinize a picture and then asked them a set of sixty questions which were prearranged to cover all the details. The students knew the object of the experiment and were told not to attempt to answer any question about which they felt uncertain. After giving each answer, they indicated whether they would be prepared to take an oath as to its accuracy or whether they were only moderately certain about it. They were given the same interrogation on four different occasions: immediately after seeing the picture, five days after, fifteen days after, and forty-five days after. The main results were as follows.

Number of days since experience	0	5	15	45
Average number of questions answered	59	57	57	57
Average number of wrong answers	8	10	12	13
Average number of questions answered and sworn to	42	39	38	35
Average number of wrong sworn answers	3	4	6	7

The number of wrong answers is, it is true, small but, in a court of law, it might be just those answers which would tip the balance of a final judgement.

In summary of this section, it may be said that errors of testimony are almost unavoidable and that, while interrogation is an excellent means of filling out the gaps in spontaneous report, it has its dangers. It leads witnesses, especially children and unsophisticated adults, into false deposition. Falsification can be reduced, but not completely eliminated, by: asking for sworn testimony; obtaining the testimony as soon after the event as possible; and confining the testimony to that given in a spontaneous report and in answer to questions which are framed as non-suggestively as possible.

4. RUMOURS AND FOLK-TALES

In an earlier section, it was indicated that the results obtained by the Method of Serial Reproduction are of interest in two major respects. They illustrate the distortions which occur in long-term remembering; and they represent an analogy to the way in which rumours and folk-tales grow and change in the growing. A rumour may be broadly defined as information, purporting to be about some real event, which is passed on from person to person, usually by word of mouth, without secure standards of evidence being present. We are all familiar with rumours, both complimentary and scandalous. Typically, they have a fairly well identified central figure such as Professor X or the Government; they specify fairly clearly the character of the action, the destructiveness, the meanness, the benificence which gives the tone to the story; and their source is vague, whether it be an insubstantial 'they' or an equally elusive 'good authority'. Rumours are, despite their social importance, short-lived. They rise, circulate for a few days or weeks or months, then disappear when they are no longer topical. Folk-tales, on the other hand, possess remarkable longevity. Whether they deal with the mundane or the supernatural, whether they preserve in oral tradition the deeds of long ago or explain why this house is uninhabited or how the bear lost his tail, they appeal to long-term interests. They are rumours which have persisted to become part of the verbal heritage of a people.

It is obvious that both rumours and folk-tales merit mention in any book devoted to memory. And for this reason, the present section is devoted to these social phenomena. But an exhaustive discussion would be out of place – it would lead us too far into the fields of social psychology and anthropology. The main outlines can be found in *The Psychology of Rumor*, a readable little book published in America by Gordon W. Allport and Leo Postman in 1947. Here, we shall discuss only those aspects of rumours and folk-tales which are of direct relevance to the psychology of memory.

We have seen that, as 'The War of The Ghosts' passed from mouth to mouth, there was such a change of emphasis, such a cumulation of omissions, transpositions, and inventions that the original became barely recognizable. We have also seen that the transformations in this laboratory-created rumour were the result of interpretation, of the unwitting effort of each member of the chain to make sense of the story. Now, exactly the same sorts of changes seem to occur in rumour. However, it should be realized that, despite their superficial similarity, there are three main points of difference between rumour as it is produced in the laboratory and as it occurs in real life. The first difference relates to the individual's concern with accuracy. Subjects participating in a serial reproduction experiment are instructed beforehand to recount the story as accurately as possible. These instructions produce a restraint. They diminish the exaggeration which stems from a person's attempts to impress his audience either with the drama of the tale or with the extent to which he is 'in the know' regarding information not accessible to his hearers. They also check the more or less deliberate addition of gratuitous interpretations of the kind prefaced by phrases such as 'But if you ask me what really happened ...' In the social setting which is the medium for rumour, such restraint is absent. The second difference between the laboratory and the real-life rumour concerns the time which elapses between the individual's hearing of the story and his retelling it In the laboratory, the time interval is usually negligible. In real life, this time lapse is variable and may be sufficiently long to enable the additional forgetting of details and the further introduction of distortions to take place. The third, and by far the most important, difference between the two situations is the motivation of the individuals concerned. The laboratory situation is relatively impersonal. The story has no intimate bearing on the lives of the subjects, and is repeated by them, not because of its interest but merely to comply with the experimenter's instructions. The motivation involved in listening to and passing on the story is the most distinctive characteristic of rumours and folk-tales. And something must now be said about it.

For a rumour to thrive, its theme must be of some importance to both speaker and listener and, also, the true facts must be shrouded in some sort of ambiguity. Neither importance nor ambiguity is, by itself, sufficient. If the government announces an increase in income tax and this increase is reliably reported to us through the newspapers and over the radio, rumours do not spring up regarding the increase, or at least regarding the increase as such: the event is important to most of us but it is not ambiguous. If changes occur in the market price of camels in Afghanistan, we are not likely to hear rumours about it: the event is ambiguous but is, as far as we are concerned, unimportant.

The fact that rumours depend on the ambiguity of important events means that they will be more prevalent in some situations than in others. They will not occur in intimate, settled groups of people who know one another so well that, despite gossip and endless discussion, a bizarre story concerning one of them will not be accepted and passed on. They will occur in situations where no one knows exactly what is happening and where the human need to know makes any aspect of that situation good conversation. This is apparent during wars, strikes, and times of social crisis generally. It is also seen in large factories, schools, offices, and hospitals where little is known about the private lives and doings of those important people who wield administrative power. It follows that at least one method of arresting the growth of rumour is to remove ambiguity by supplying adequate information. If this information comes from a trusted source and is accepted by a group of people, then the rumour is scotched for this group.

The fact that rumours depend on the importance of ambiguous events means that a rumour which circulates widely through one section of society may not appear in others. Teachers, lawyers, bankers, tea clubs, and bridge parties all have their own set of rumours concerning these events which, for the particular group, are important enough to compete in the rivalry of general conversation. When we say that rumours circulate only where the story has importance for the members of the rumour-chain, we are drawing attention to the motivational factor. Any human motive, or more usually combination of motives, may be at work. Sex interest operates through much of gossip and most of scandal: anxiety is at work behind the macabre and threatening tales of disaster or impending disaster: hopes and desires underlie pipe-dream rumours: hate and jealousy sustain accusing tales. Rumour often gives verbal outlet and relief to our emotional tensions, enabling us to express our antipathies, fears, and desires. And, at the same time, it serves to justify us in feeling the way we do. It is often a subtle and metaphorical way of saying: 'Why shouldn't I dislike so-and-so? He got the job I wanted by unfair means,' or 'Why shouldn't I feel superior? I don't behave in the outrageous way that he does,' or 'Why shouldn't I feel optimistic?

Other people like me have had lucky breaks.' Thus, they often protect and justify those attitudes which, if faced directly, might be distasteful to us. Apart from this emotional aspect, rumour also serves our need to understand events, to know just what is happening, and to find a reasonable explanation for it. We need to know the why, how, and wherefore of the surrounding world, and especially those features of it which are likely to affect us personally. And, as a substitute for reliable but unavailable news, curiosity rumours result. A stranger who has just come to live in our neighbourhood will soon become the subject of rumours which would explain who he is and why he has come. In short, nothing could be further from the truth than to describe rumours as idle. They are motivated in a complex way which is seldom, if ever, clearly understood by the rumour spreader and is difficult enough for even the psychologist to understand. This much, however, is certain. Any rumour serves one or more of at least four distinct functions. It may serve a social purpose in giving the story teller the attention of the group, a moment of conversational leadership. It may relieve our emotional tension. It may justify us in holding the attitudes we do. And it may render the surrounding world intelligible.

As compared with rumour, the folk-tale has the additional distinction of treating issues which are of more than transitory importance. Like the rumour, it undergoes transformation until it assumes a relatively stereotyped form couched in simple and concrete terms. It is not expressed in abstract language but recounts specific happenings of a familiar or, at least, readily intelligible kind. The tale does not, however, owe its persistence so much to the specific circumstances it recounts as to its considerable metaphorical significance. Both teller and hearer may be aware that it contains no literal truth. But this is not important if it is metaphorically true. The Christmas rose, despite snow and ice, is said to burst into blossom at midnight on Christmas Eve: it may not do so in fact, but it might well as an expression of the gladness of that season. The folk-tale, like the great work of literary fiction, expresses through specific characters and concrete happenings the fears and wishes and problems which are common to every member of a particular society. For example, the mighty Icelandic Sagas supply a sense of stability and comradeship and a pride of ancestry. The deeds of their heroes and villains embody the universal and recurring features of human personality. Their account of the world's creation, of the seasons, and of the caprices of the gods furnish a plausible explanation of these cosmic riddles which are the most important and yet the most eternally ambiguous faced by man in his brief and confusing existence.

The differences between the rumour, the folk-tale, and the serial reproduction experiment have now been indicated. What of their similarities ? It is difficult to obtain the detailed history of a rumour. It is more difficult still to trace the progress of a folk-tale. But what evidence there is suggests that all three phenomena follow the same basic pattern. Each undergoes progressive transformation in being passed on from individual to individual. Each takes on a form which is more intelligible and meaningful to the members of the group among which it passes. And each assumes this form by being assimilated to the schemata of each person concerned – schemata which have been built up over his lifetime and reflect his individual needs, preoccupations, fears, and doubts along with the attitudes and interests which he has acquired from the social group in which he lives. We may conclude this discussion of rumours and folk-tales by giving two examples of transformation.

Our first example illustrates the progressive distortion of 'history' by a succession of writers who rely on each other's interpretations rather than on the original evidence. This example is taken from a booklet published in 1956 by The Historical Association. The event is the signing of the National Covenant in Edinburgh in the year 1638 – an event which has aroused heated partisanship even up to the present day. The popular account of the signing is that, on 28 February, the people of Edinburgh thronged into Greyfriars Church and overflowed into the churchyard to append their names, even in blood from their veins, to copies of the Covenant spread out on flat tombstones. This account is a simplified and dramatized version of the more complex and sober historical

reality. What actually happened was that, on the day mentioned, there was only one copy of the Covenant which was
subscribed in the church between 4 and 8 p.m. by some 150
to 200 nobles and gentlemen. On the following day, more
copies were available in another part of Edinburgh for signing
by nobles, clergy, and commissioners of burghs. The 'people
of Edinburgh' did not sign till later and, when they did, it was
neither in Greyfriars church nor in the churchyard. The stone
traditionally associated with the event is, in fact, of a much
later date than 1638. The popular account then continues to
add that the first person to sign was the aged and sickly Earl of
Sutherland, and we are given a picture of a life crowded with
wisdom and nobility and crowned by one last defiant gesture.
'Accounts of the event illustrate the growth of a legend,
because James Gordon in his *History of Scots Affairs* narrates
that the first to subscribe was John Gordon, Earl of Sutherland: Robert Chambers, in *History of the Rebellions in
Scotland*, added these words: "a nobleman venerable for his
excellent domestic character"; Rev. John Aiton, in *Life and
Times of Alexander Henderson* (1836), refers to him as "the
venerable Earl of Sutherland"; Hetherington, in his *History of
the Church of Scotland*, speaks of "an aged nobleman, the
venerable Earl of Sutherland," stepping "slowly and reveren-
tially forward" and subscribing "with throbbing heart and
trembling hand." The object of all this veneration was under
29 years of age!'

Our second example illustrates how a folk-tale may be
radically changed in passing from one cultural context to
another. In Northern Europe, the bear is one of the few
animals which does not possess a tail, and we find a folk-story
to explain how it was lost. One winter night, it is said, the fox
persuaded the bear to dip his tail into the water in order to
catch fish: the water froze: and, in pulling himself free, the
bear left his tail behind and so lost it for ever. This story
spread into southern countries and, in being assimilated by
members of a different region, underwent transformation. In
these countries there are no bears, and the story is told as one
of several concerning the cunning of the fox. In place of the
unknown bear, the familiar wolf is substituted. And, although

the wolf does have a tail, this is a minor detail which does not affect the central theme which has now become concerned with the characteristic cunning of the fox.

In summary of this whole chapter, it may be said that the recall of stories and events is rarely accurate. There are omissions, transpositions, and additions resulting from interpretation, from the individual's making the account conform to his standards of intelligibility. Thus, recall is often less a matter of literal reproduction than of the imaginative construction of fragmentary recall into a coherent whole. Normally the individual is unaware of this constructive characteristic of his remembering. But on occasion, especially in the retelling of rumours and folk-tales, he may interpret deliberately in order to heighten the drama of the story and capture the attention of his audience.

CHAPTER FIVE

REPRESSING

1. REPRESSION IN ABNORMAL BEHAVIOUR

In Chapter Three, some attempt was made to characterize the factors responsible for forgetting, and it was mentioned that one factor remained to be considered, namely, that of repressing. As far as memory is concerned, repressing can be defined as the unconscious blocking of the recall of those experiences and actions which have either immediate or remote potentialities for causing pain. This process got its name and its first clear recognition from Sigmund Freud, the famous Viennese physician and psychologist, who made his discovery while observing and trying to cure patients suffering from behaviour disabilities. It should be realized that the process of repressing, like that of forgetting itself, cannot be observed directly but has to be inferred from what people do and say. However, about its existence and importance there can be no shadow of doubt. The observations of Freud and of his medical and psychological successors have firmly established its reality. Freud himself devised an elaborate theoretical explanation of repression and, although this theory has never gained widespread acceptance, it has been recognized that, as Freud insisted, repression has adaptive value and is also a common predisposing factor in the development of behaviour pathology. In this chapter no attempt will be made to present Freud's theory of repression or to trace out the relationship between repression and various forms of mental illness. We shall begin by simply presenting some of the evidence for the unconscious emotional blocking of remembering. It is only fitting that this evidence should be selected from the field of abnormal behaviour, because it was from this field that the recognition of repression came, and it is still to this field that we must turn for the clearest examples of this type of forgetting. We will then raise the important question of the role played by repression in everyday life.

'The essence of repression,' said Freud, 'lies simply in the function of rejecting and keeping something out of consciousness.' The process can best be introduced by giving an example. The following quotation is taken from a book, *The Psychology of Abnormal People*, by J. J. B. Morgan and G. D. Lovell. It summarizes a case treated by Pierre Janet, a Parisian psychiatrist and a contemporary of Freud, and illustrates vividly the emotional blocking of recall.

Irene was a girl of twenty years, who was greatly disturbed by the long illness and death of her mother. Her mother had reached the last stage of tuberculosis, and lived alone in abject poverty with her daughter, in an attic. The girl watched her mother during sixty days and nights, working at her sewing machine to earn a few pennies to sustain their lives. When finally her mother did die, Irene became very much disturbed emotionally. She tried to revive the corpse, to call the breath back again. In her attempts at placing the limbs in an upright position, the mother's body fell to the floor, whereupon she were through the strain of lifting her back into bed, alone. Certainly, such experiences could not be forgotten in the ordinary course of things. Yet in a little while Irene seemed to have grown forgetful of her mother's death. She would say, 'I know very well my mother must be dead, since I have been told so several times, since I see her no more, and since I am in mourning; but I really feel astonished at it all. When did she die? What did she die from? Was I not by her to take care of her? There is something I do not understand. Why, loving her as I did, do I not feel more sorrow for her death? I can't grieve; I feel as if her absence was nothing to me, as if she were travelling, and would soon come back.' The same thing happened if you put to her questions about any of the events that happened during those two months before her mother's death. If you asked her about the illness, the mishaps, the nightly staying up, anxieties about money, the quarrels with her drunken father, – all these things seemed to have quite vanished from her mind. What had happened to her? Had something happened to her nervous system to wipe away all traces of the horrible events she had experienced? Was she simply pretending she did not remember? Or, did she remember without being able to recall, owing to some powerful inhibitions? Some light is thrown on this question by a study of the crises (or fits) which she began to experience some time after her mother's death. These would last for hours at a time, and during them she would lose contact with her immediate surroundings and perform scenes with the skill of an actress. She would re-enact all the events that took place at her mother's death, as well as other unpleasant episodes in her life, all with the greatest detail. She would carry out with words and acts the different events, and when death finally came to her mother would prepare for her own suicide. She would discuss it aloud, seem to speak to her mother, and to receive advice from her. She fancied that she would try to be run over by a locomotive. She acted as though she were on the way, and stretched herself out on the floor of the room, waiting with dread and impatience for death to come. She posed in true dramatic style waiting for the train to come. Finally, when it came she would utter a terrible shriek, and fall back motionless, as if she were dead. Then she would get up and begin acting over again one of the previous scenes. After a time the agitation seemed to die down and she came back to normal consciousness, took up her ordinary business, seemingly quite undisturbed about what had happened and with the concomitant loss of memory for the events she has so faithfully dramatized.

In the above case, we can readily see what is meant by emotional blocking of recall. Irene's experiences had been so harrowing that the recollecting of them was unbearable and could be escaped from only by committing suicide (which she nearly did) or by forming this inhibitory block against recall. When the strong tendency to recall could no longer be inhibited, recall occurred – but at the expense of her waking consciousness so that she went into the 'crises' described. Notice also that it was not only the recollecting of the events of her mother's death which was blocked, but of everything related to these events. The recall of any subsidiary but related event was likewise denied entry into consciousness.

Repressive forgetting can manifest itself in a bewildering variety of ways. But in all cases, there are certain common features which are illustrated in the above account. First, there is no question of the original experience not being adequately impressed on the patient and retained by him. Eventually, recall can occur, either spontaneously or as a result of special treatment (involving drugs, 'free association', or hypnosis). Second, recall cannot occur either in consequence of being questioned or of making a voluntary attempt to remember. However hard the patient may try, he cannot recall. It is this which differentiates repressing from the moderate forgetting which can be brought about by the common techniques of avoidance and distraction. The recall of an unpleasant experience can be, to some extent, checked by avoiding reintegrating circumstances, that is, places and topics which are associated with it and so remind us of it. Recall can also be checked by 'losing ourselves' in pursuits which distract and absorb our attention. But however effective these techniques may be, they are never so successful that we cannot recall the experience when we make an attempt to do so. With repressing, on the other hand, voluntary attempts at recall are of no avail. It is noteworthy, however, that these attempts are often far from strenuous. Although nothing can actually be recalled, the attempt seems to be unpleasant and is often interrupted by such signs of emotion as anxiety, nausea, and the sudden onset of headache. Third, the repressed experiences always turn out to involve deeply disturbing anxiety. They may involve some unresolved and perplexing conflict, or some anticipation of unwelcome punishment, or some strong threat to self-regard. They may arouse the strong emotional reactions of fear, guilt, shame, disgust, sorrow, or feelings of inferiority. But always, without exception, the repressed experiences are such as to arouse, when recalled, some extremely unpleasant emotional reaction. The utility of repression to the patient is, of course, the very avoidance of this emotional upset. Fourth, repression is not only an active process but a continuous one. According to Freud, it is not an act which merely occurs once and disposes of the problem forever: the blocking requires a constant expenditure of energy on the patient's part and may even, in itself, be exhausting. Support is lent to this view by the fact that the repressed experiences can eventually be recollected with surprising vividness and also by the fact that they not infrequently break through the inhibitory block either in a disguised form or at the expense of conscious awareness. This loss of normal consciousness is what happened in Irene's 'crises' (and fiction provides us with the instance of Shakespeare's Lady Macbeth). It is also evident in many cases of soldiers who have forgotten all about some harrowing war-time experience and yet, during sleep, re-enact this same repressed incident. On waking, they are, like Irene, characteristically unaware of their somnambulism. The repressed experiences may have gained overt expression but, again, they have been kept out of consciousness.

Having outlined the main characteristics of repressing, it must now be repeated that what is repressed varies markedly from patient to patient. It may be the recollection of all experiences which occurred over a particular long or short period of time. It may be the recollection of all experiences related to a certain event or sphere of activity. It may be only a name, or a word, or a phrase. And it may not only be the recollection but also the recall (performance) of definite motor habits such as how to write, or sew, or drive a car, or make a bed. The patient may even forget how to stand or walk, although he has not lost the ability to use his legs in other ways. In short, repressing may involve the blocking off of any past experience or learned performance and the resulting loss may be either slight or extensive. Popular interest has, understandably enough, centred round those dramatic cases where the loss has been one of personal identity. Indeed, the term 'amnesia' – which, strictly speaking, applies to all forms of pathological forgetting whether produced by drugs, brain injury, or repression – has been captured by the newspaper press to refer to just this special, and not too common, type of memory disorder. Loss of personal identity is found in the conditions of 'fugue' and 'multiple personality'. Because these conditions have aroused such widespread curiosity and because they further illustrate the emotional blocking of recall, they will now be briefly discussed.

2. LOSS OF PERSONAL INDENTITY

The term 'fugue' literally means 'flight'. It is used to refer to an extended episode of acting as a 'different person'. A particularly clear case of this condition was described many years ago by the British psychologist, William McDougall.

During active war-service, a colour-sergeant was entrusted with the delivery of a message and was riding his motorcycle through a dangerous sector of the front. All at once – or so it seemed – it was several hours later and he found himself pushing his cycle along the streets of a coastal town nearly a hundred miles away. This town was, incidentally, a port from which soldiers embarked for home. He was startled and bewildered by this and, as often happens in such cases, he gave himself into the hands of the police. He could recall nothing of his long trip but, eventually, under medical treatment, he was able to recollect being thrown down by a shell explosion, picking himself up, getting on to his machine, starting straight for the coastal town, and reading signposts and asking directions in order to reach his destination. As far as he could recollect, he had thought of nothing other than reaching this coastal town: every action and thought had been subordinated to this goal. His condition during the flight had been not unlike that of a normal person who is so absorbed in some task as to be oblivious and 'absent-minded' of his surroundings. What seems to have happened was that he had been in conflict between fear, suddenly intensified by his narrow escape, and duty to complete the dangerous mission. The forgetting of his personal identity – of who he was and what he was doing – enabled him to resolve this conflict by giving way to flight while not exposing himself to the almost equally unbearable anxiety of being a coward, failing his mission, and undergoing arrest as a deserter. Once he had gained the safety of the coastal town, the two sides of his conflict resumed normal proportions and his sense of personal identity returned abruptly as though he were waking from a dream. With this return of identity came the characteristic amnesia for the experiences of the flight itself.

In times of war, there are many cases of fugue which, like that above, originate under suddenly violent circumstances. In civilian life, fugue often occurs under conditions which are seemingly free from any disturbance. Someone goes out for a walk and is suddenly bewildered to find himself a complete stranger in strange surroundings: he recognizes none of the once familiar faces around him, he has no idea of his name, of his occupation, of whether he is married or not, of his home. In this amnesic state, he often turns to the police or to a hospital for help. On examination, he is found to be quite normal in every respect. His only peculiarity is that, however hard and genuinely he may try, he can recall nothing which will enable either the physician or himself to arrive at his identity. Usually the patient returns, either spontaneously or with medical assistance, to his normal state and is surprised to find himself in hospital for, now, he can recall nothing of the amnesic episode and has no recollection of how he came to be where he is.

These cases of fugue are not well understood. But wherever they have been investigated thoroughly, they have been found to possess one characteristic in common. The significant precipitating factor is some intensely unpleasant conflict amounting to an emotional crisis in the individual's life. The conflict may be concerned with finance or family, with escape from danger or threatened punishment. And, in the fugue, the patient translates into overt behaviour his need to 'get away from it all'. He blocks off all those innumerable experiences which would bring him back into the conflict situation. Notice, however, that this forgetting is highly selective. He forgets everything which makes him the unique social individual, the Mr X, which he is. But he does not necessarily forget how to speak, how to understand language, write, drive a car, and so on. The consequence of this selective forgetting may well be called fugue. The patient flees, either literally or metaphorically, from his unbearable circumstances. He takes refuge in amnesia from those conflicts which he is incapable of resolving as long as he retains his sense of social identity.

This very brief account of fugue raises one important question. Many people find themselves in a state of acute and unresolved conflict. But not all of them gain relief by repressing their personal identity. Why should one individual 'resort' to fugue, another to suicide, and another to any one of the many forms of so-called nervous breakdown ? This, unfortunately, is a question to which there are, as yet, no satisfactory answers. Just what subtle combination of hereditary and environmental influences predisposes an individual to this or that type of mental illness is yet another of those problems which are currently being investigated by psychologists and psychiatrists. It is yet another of those socially important problems on which evidence is beginning to accumulate but which is still far from being solved. Only this much has become apparent. The answer, when and if it does emerge, will be far from simple.

In fugue, the individual becomes, to some extent, a 'different person'. But this 'different person' is lacking in identity, confused, bewildered, agitated, and quite clearly not normal. In multiple personality, on the other hand, the 'different person' has an identity and a self-consistency of expression and behaviour which, superficially at least, makes him an acceptable and balanced social being. Multiple personality refers to that condition where the individual possesses two or more 'personalities' each of which is so well developed and integrated as to have a relatively rich, unified, and stable life of its own. In 1944, two American psychologists, W. S. Taylor and M. F. Martin, undertook to collect and classify all available case records of such multiple personality, and their labours revealed three significant facts. First, there can be no doubt about the genuineness of the condition. It is true that some people may intentionally behave in very different ways at different times. They may even act out an elaborate impersonation. But such intentional deception does not detract from the genuine occurrence of multiple personality any more than the simulated amnesia or bodily illness of the malingerer detracts from the reality of amnesia or illness generally. Skilful examination can usually detect the fraud from the genuine case. Second, multiple personality occurs much less frequently than its literary exploitation would suggest. The extensive search revealed that, out of the thousands upon thousands of recorded cases of behaviour disorder, there were only seventy-six available records of multiple personality. It was estimated that perhaps no more than 150 cases have appeared in the voluminous bulk of the world's medical and psychological case records. Third, the condition manifests itself in such a variety of forms as to defy any brief summing up, since no two cases are quite the same.

Multiple personality clearly differs in degree rather than in kind from the less dramatic dissociation found in day dreaming, play acting, restlessness during sleep, and somnambulism (sleep walking). And many of the cases can be seen as developing out of fugue. After losing his sense of personal identity, the subject does not remain disorientated and neither does he resume his customary orientation. He picks up, as it were, the threads of a new existence. He begins to build up for himself a disparate, protective role. His new phase of existence can be called a role, or even a personality, since it is a way of life which is fairly self-consistent. This role is disparate in that it represents a sharp discontinuity in his living which is more or less opposed to, and separate from, the rest of his personality. And this new role is protective since, in it, the individual can escape from his conflicts and anxieties and so feel more secure than he could feel otherwise. The new role may be developed gradually or it may already have been built up by fantasy and be ready for him to step into. He may become the sort of person he has often consciously wished to become. He may behave like a baby, or a child, or a peaceful person, or a thief, or a sailor, or like any one real or imagined person. Whatever the role, he learns more and more reactions to augment it until, circumstances permitting, the role becomes sufficiently strong and rich to emerge as a complete way of life. He has a new identity and occupation, new friends and leisure pursuits and, to casual observers, appears quite normal.

While the new role is being developed and maintained, there is, of course, repression of all or many of those recollections which would supply the individual with his former identity. Often after living successfully in this partially amnesic state, sometimes for years, he suddenly and spontaneously returns to his previous condition and, now, may recollect nothing of his second role. He then resumes his former way of living as best he can, and that may be the end of the episode. But, in some cases, there is a later return of the second role and perhaps an alternation between it and the first. Such alternating personalities may be 'mutually amnesic', that is, the different personalities can remember nothing of each other's experiences and activities. It is this type which was so skilfully dramatized by Robert Louis Stevenson in his fictional case of Dr Jekyll and Mr Hyde. Alternatively, there may be 'one-way' amnesia where personality X recollects none of Y's experiences but Y remembers all of X's. There may even be a 'coconscious personality' which continues to function subconsciously while the other is dominant and functioning consciously. This 'coconscious personality' indicates its presence in some roundabout way such as in 'automatic writing' where the patient may be carrying on a normal conversation as X while his hand writes, without his being aware of it, messages of a style and content quite different from both his consciously controlled writing and his present topic of conversation. In these very rare cases (Taylor and Martin discovered records of only twenty-seven) where there are more than two distinct personalities, certain roles may be mutually amnesic while others are one-way amnesic. Thus, different types of organization may be combined within a single case.

This section may be concluded by quoting Taylor and Martin's description of what appears to be the earliest well documented case of multiple personality.

Mary Reynolds was born in England in 1793, and was brought to Pennsylvania by her family when she was four years old. The girl was intelligent. She grew up in a strongly religious atmosphere, and became melancholy, shy, and given to solitary religious devotions and meditations. She was considered normal until she was about eighteen. Then she began to have occasional 'fits', which were evidently hysterical. One of these attacks, when she was about nineteen years old, left her blind and deaf for five or six weeks. Some three months later, she slept eighteen or twenty hours, and awoke seeming to know scarcely anything that she had learned. She soon became acquainted with her surroundings, however, and within a few weeks learned reading, calculating, and writing, though her penmanship was crude compared to what it had been. Now she was buoyant, witty, fond of company and a lover of nature. After five weeks of this new life, she slept long again, and awoke as her 'normal' self, with no memory for what she had experienced since her recent lapse. Thereafter the 'new' or 'second state' and the 'old' or 'first state' ... alternated irregularly. The second state gained over the first, however, and became more rich and stable, until the woman was about thirty-six years old. At that time the second state became permanent and continued until her death in 1854.

3. REPRESSION IN NORMAL BEHAVIOUR

Does repressing, so dramatically evident in the mentally ill, play any part in the everyday forgetting of normal people ? This is the question to which the remainder of this chapter will be devoted, and it may be said at the outset that it is not an easy question to answer. It is of no avail to seek the answer in our personal experience of our own behaviour. Search our past history as we may, we will find no evidence of repressive forgetting, since this is, by its very nature, something of which we are not aware. We cannot repress the recollection of an experience and, at the same time, be aware that we are doing so. Where then should we turn for evidence ? Freud would claim that the evidence is forthcoming from at least three sources, namely, the results of 'free association', the everyday forgetting of names and words, and the fact of 'infantile amnesia'. We may now examine these three sources of evidence in turn. What we will find is that: the first answers our question in the affirmative; the second is doubtful but, in some cases, suggestive of repression; and the third is more easily explained in terms which make no recourse to repression.

Free Association. It was earlier mentioned that we can recall more than we usually imagine ourselves capable of doing. If we persist in trying to recall a poem which we once knew but have since forgotten, we can gradually recall more and more. Now the Freudian technique of free association is, in a sense, an effort which is continued over months, or even years, to recall more and more of our past experiences. For reasons which need not be discussed here, it is one of the aims of psycho-analysis to recover repressed experiences. The manner of doing this was evolved by Freud as a result of much trial and error and is, in outline, simple. Instead of trying to elicit recall by hypnotism or any other form of suggestion, or by urging the patient to recall experiences of a particular kind, the patient is asked to relax and say 'whatever comes into his head'. He must report everything as it occurs to him and make no attempt to hold anything back in the interests of logic or decency. It is perhaps inaccurate to call this a process of 'free' association for, while it is free from many conventional restraints, it is not free in the way that idle reverie is free. In the first place, the patient is suffering from some disturbance and has come to be cured. This circumstance dominates the whole situation and inevitably exerts its influence on the course of the associations. In the second place, the thoughts and recollections must be communicated to a listener, and this at once brings into play our life-long habits of suppressing certain topics and trying to 'put up a good front'. It is by no means easy to express in words every idea that drifts through our head, and it may require weeks or months of practice before we can learn to verbalize these ideas and bring ourselves to do so without reserve. There is a resistance against telling everything and all sorts of excuses are given for not doing so; for example, there is nothing to tell, or it is too silly or trivial. But this resistance does not go on for ever. The patient is encouraged by the analyst, who points out similarities between this and that recollected experience or thought. He gains confidence in the analyst's sympathy, coming to accept that he will not criticize or be shocked by anything that is said. He accepts that the analyst will comfort him and help him to deal with his anxieties. And he abandons himself to free expression. Sometimes, he reports events and feelings of which he has been aware for some time but has never been willing to express in words. But he is more and more likely to find himself recalling experiences which he had hitherto been unaware of having had. That the recollection of these experiences had been repressed is indicated by the fact that they are recollected not piecemeal but as a whole, not dimly but extremely vividly, and are accompanied by strongly unpleasant emotional reactions. They often, but not always, have the further characteristic of being directly related to some present behaviour disturbance. There seems little doubt that the recollection of these experiences had, until this time, been blocked from consciousness.

Such instances of repression are reported uniformly in the case records of psycho-analysts in such a way that we must accept their authenticity. Granting, then, that free association always reveals repression, this helps us to answer our question, since many of the 'patients' have been normal adults. Psycho-analysis was developed as a method of treating neurotics. But it has also been undergone by people who are, if anything, better adjusted and more stable than the general run of the population. Most of them have been people who wished to become psycho-analysts themselves, and a few have been psychologists who have simply wanted to discover exactly what the technique involves. Now, if these normal people have been found to 'employ' repression, it seems highly likely that we do so too. Thus, the results of free association suggest that repressive forgetting has occurred in the lives of all of us with regard to those experiences the recollection of which would cause us acute anxiety. We all block the recalling of some unpleasant past experiences and our lives are the happier and the better for it.

Everyday Forgetting. In 1914, Freud published an English edition of his *The Psychopathology of Everyday Life*. In this book he endeavours to show that many 'lapses of memory' and 'slips of the tongue' are not inexplicable accidents but can be readily understood if fitted into the personality picture of the individual. The reader is recommended to look at this well-written book for himself and discover the wealth of intriguing anecdotal evidence with which Freud supports and develops his thesis.

Freud is at his best when discussing those seemingly accidental mistakes of speech and writing where one word is substituted for another and, especially, where the substitute word means the opposite of the word intended. A physician is writing out a prescription for an impecunious patient who asks him not to give her big bills because she cannot swallow them – and then says that, of course, she meant pills. An arrogant lecturer says that he could count the number of real authorities on his subject on one finger – he means the fingers of one hand. A President of the Austrian House of Deputies is

opening a session from which he fears little good will come
and announces that, since such and such a number of gentlemen are present, he declares the session as closed; amid
laughter, he corrects his mistake and declares the session as
opened. All of these examples clearly derive from the person
saying what he actually thinks without checking himself in
time to make his insincere but diplomatic statement. No
doubt we have all encountered similar examples in our everyday life. Certainly, writers of fiction have long been aware of
this phenomenon, and have exploited it to good dramatic
effect by putting such *lapsus linguae* in the mouths of their
characters. In Shakespeare's *Merchant of Venice*, for example,
Portia has lost her affections to Bassanio but is under a vow
not to reveal it. She directs a speech to this welcome suitor in
which, throughout, her love for him is thinly disguised and
finishes with the words: 'One half of me is yours, the other
half yours – Mine own, I would say.' The same expression of
our thoughts and wishes is seen in some erroneously carried-
out actions. Thus, one physician reports that he is quite often
disturbed in the midst of engrossing work at home by having
to go to hospital to carry out some routine duty. When this
happens, he is apt to find himself trying to open the door of
his laboratory with the key of his desk at home. The two keys
are quite unlike each other and the mistake does not occur
under normal circumstances but only under conditions where
he would rather be at home. His error seems to express this
wish.

When Freud begins to discuss 'lapses of memory' in terms
of repression, he seems to move on to less firm ground. He
does not, of course, claim that all lapses are due to repression.
His concern is to show that at least some are and, to this end,
he gives examples in which a name or word is unexpectedly
forgotten and proceeds to demonstrate that the forgotten item
is associated either directly or indirectly with unpleasant
circumstances. Here we may cite two of his most convincing
examples. The first concerns a man (X) who repeatedly forgot
the name of an old acquaintance and business associate (Y).
When he required to correspond with Y, he had to ask other
people for his name. It transpired that Y had recently married

a young woman whom X himself had hoped to marry. Thus, X had good reason to dislike his happy rival and want to forget all about him. The second example concerns a man who set out to recite a poem, got so far, and then could recall no more although he knew the poem well. The line on which he blocked was descriptive of a pine-tree which is covered 'with the white sheet'. Why should this phrase have been forgotten ? Asked to relate what came to mind when he thought of this phrase, it was found that it immediately reminded him of the white sheet which covers a dead body, and of the recent death of his brother from a heart condition which was common in his family and from which he feared he too might die. The phrase referring to the white sheet appears to have been forgotten because it was associated with circumstances which the man did not wish to recall. In Freud's other examples, the link between the forgotten item and some unpleasant circumstance is not so easily demonstrated. The 'subject' (often Freud himself) considers the item, keeps on telling what it suggests to him and, sooner or later, reports some unpleasant association. This, says Freud, is the explanation. The item was 'deliberately' forgotten because it was associated with this unpleasant experience the conscious recollection of which would have been painful. Now, Freud's analysis of these examples may be correct. They may, on the other hand, be more ingenious than veridical. And there seems to be no definite way of deciding. His whole case seems to rest on an often tortuous association between the forgotten item and a painful experience. Any critic could start with any word whatever and trace a link, no less indirect than those traced by Freud, to an unpleasant experience. It would be possible for him to match each of Freud's examples with a case in which he takes a word which is not forgotten by an individual, traces it to some unpleasant experience which that individual has had, and so explains why (although the word was recalled) it ought really to have been forgotten. In short, the great bulk of Freud's examples, while ingenious and suggestive, are unconvincing when we realize the highly selective nature of the argument he invokes. It may, in fact, be that a temporary inability to recall a word is due to our not really wanting to recall it. It may be that an object is misplaced because we really want to lose it. But, at the moment, there is no evidence to suggest that this is anything more than a plausible hypothesis.

4. RECOLLECTING CHILDHOOD EXPERIENCES

We can recollect remarkably little of our early childhood experiences. Why should this be so ? Freud's suggestion is that the recollection of these early experiences is repressed because they are so intimately associated with the primitive, selfish, pleasure-seeking tendencies of early childhood; tendencies which were initially repressed because they met with punishment and parental disaffection; tendencies which are denied present expression because they would be so painfully inconsistent with our socially-derived notions of the sort of person we are and the way we should behave. Freud and others have accumulated much evidence to show that infants and pre-school children have many strong (and sometimes 'sexual') behaviour tendencies which are, somehow or other, eliminated in the lengthy process of learning to be socially acceptable beings. It may be that much of this elimination is achieved by repressing. If this were so, then early childhood would be the time, above all others, for repression and it would not be surprising that we should have forgotten all about our early nonconforming tendencies and the experiences associated with them. In the face of present-day knowledge about child development, this suggestion of Freud's is by no means as fantastic as it might appear at first sight. It is a hypothesis which must be considered seriously. Let us now try to see how it squares with the facts of 'infantile amnesia'.

In setting out to investigate the recollection of childhood experiences, our greatest difficulty lies in obtaining authentic recollection. Recall of events is, as we have seen, susceptible to considerable distortion, particularly events which occurred a long time before. There is also the possibility that the recollection may not be genuine and that the account is based on stories of his own past which the individual has heard so often that he has come to believe erroneously that he can actually recollect the event concerned. It may be said at the outset that there is no way of guaranteeing the authenticity of the recalled events, although there are some methods of eliciting recall which are more likely to be free from errors than others. For example, a particularly unsatisfactory method would be to send out mailed questionnaires and so obtain details of the earliest experiences which can be recollected by respondents whose identity and sincerity may not always be known. Obviously, it is much better to elicit recall by direct (but non-suggestive) questioning and, if possible, check the accounts with relations, friends, teachers, or other witnesses of the original event. Bearing in mind, then, this inherent difficulty in the investigation of childhood memory, we may now cite a study conducted in America by S. Waldfogel in 1948 and briefly summarize the main findings as they apply to university students.

After securing the co-operation of 124 students and stressing the importance of careful and candid reporting, Waldfogel gave these young men and women eighty-five minutes in which to write down all the experiences they could recollect from their first eight years of life. They had to date each experience as accurately as possible and also state if it was one which they felt sure they had recollected spontaneously, if it was one which they had not been able to recollect but had been told about, or if they were uncertain whether or not they had recollected it. The great majority of students found that the eighty-five minute period was long enough to complete this task to their satisfaction. At the end of the period, the students were asked to re-read each event reported, consider it carefully, and indicate whether it had been very pleasant, pleasant, neutral, unpleasant, or very unpleasant. They were also asked to indicate their emotional reaction at the time of the original event. Some forty days later, this whole procedure was repeated without warning. The outcome of this second session was substantially the same as that of the first, with the notable exception that almost half as many new experiences were reported in addition to those reported before. This illustrates, once more the important point that, in any one attempt at recall, we recall less than we are, in fact, capable of recalling. This also means that we cannot speak in absolute terms about the number of events which can be recalled: we can only say that, under such and such conditions, so many experiences are recalled. In both sessions, each student was known to the experimenter only as a number in the hope that, if his identity were unknown, he would be less tempted to hold back any possibly embarrassing experiences.

Of the total number of experiences reported, some 90 per cent were indicated as having been recollected. The average number of such recollections for each student was as follows.

	Age at time of event (in years)							
	0–1	1–2	2–3	3–4	4–5	5–6	6–7	7–8
Average number of events recollected	0·0	0·1	0·7	2·8	6·8	11·3	14·0	16·5

We can see from these figures that recollections from the first three years of life are very rare and that the *average* age of the earliest experience is in the fourth year of life. Most investigators agree that, while the earliest memory may be as early as the first year or as late as the seventh, the average individual has, as his earliest recollection, an experience which occurred between the ages of three and four. The above figures also show that the number of recollected experiences increases rapidly with increasing age.

When the memories were studied in terms of their affect, it was found that the emotions which the subjects recalled as having prevailed at the time were numerous and varied. Most commonly experienced had been joy which constituted about 30 per cent of the total. Next in frequency had been fear, about 15 per cent, followed by pleasure, anger, grief, and excitement, all between 5 and 10 per cent. The recall of pleasant events was more frequent than of unpleasant or neutral events. In round numbers, pleasant memories constituted about 50 per cent of the total, unpleasant memories about 30 per cent, and neutral memories about 20 per cent.

Now there is nothing in the above findings which runs directly contrary to Freud's hypothesis. On the quantitative side, we find the small number of recollected experiences consistent with the assumption that there has been a great deal of repressing in the early years. On the qualitative side, we find the preponderance of pleasant or neutral experiences consistent with the suggestion that there has been a selective forgetting of the unpleasant. Thus, in face of the facts, Freud's repression explanation of 'infantile amnesia' holds its ground. However, before accepting Freud's explanation, we ought to consider whether the above findings might not be accounted for in terms of these more prosaic processes which have already become familiar to us in the preceding chapters of this book.

Turning first to the quantitative findings regarding the number of memories from each age level, the explanation which immediately suggests itself is that of retroactive interference. If we take the average age of Waldfogel's subjects as being twenty years, many experiences must have occurred in the twelve to twenty years between the original experiences and their recall. This might well account for the obliteration of many of those early experiences, but it seems unlikely that it would account altogether for the different number of memories from the different ages. The number of memories from fifteen years ago is more than twice that from sixteen years ago and more than nine times the number from seventeen years ago. Suppose a man of 40 were recalling his past experiences of fifteen, sixteen, and seventeen years ago, would there be an equally large difference in the number of experiences recalled? There is no definite information on this question but, on the grounds of general observation, it seems most unlikely that there would be. The years of intervening experiences would, it is true, progressively reduce the quantity recollected but, out of fifteen to seventeen years, a year here or there would probably make little difference. We would certainly not expect that our man of 40 (like these students of 20) would be unable to recall anything at all of his experiences from twenty years back. In short, retroactive interference undoubtedly plays some part in producing forgetting; but some part must also be played by the age of the individual at the time of the original experience.

It is well known that intellectual abilities in general strengthen rapidly during the childhood years. In the learning of any task, the older child, on the average, is more efficient than the younger or, to say the same thing in another way, the experiences of the younger child do not have such lasting effects. (This is not, incidentally, to deny the importance of early experience as a major determinant of the lines along which later development will occur, for this importance is due less to any individual experience than to a sequence of similar experiences.) Consider the performance of children of different ages in the testimony type of experiment. In one typical study, a picture was shown, and it was found that the average number of details later reported by three, four, five, and six year olds, respectively, was 11, 22, 35, and 44. Thus, shortly after the event, the younger children could recall less than the older children. Now, in the adult's recollecting of childhood experiences, the situation is essentially the same as in the testimony experiment (with the important difference that recall is delayed for a very much longer time) and exactly the same relation holds between age at the time of the experience and ability to recall this experience. It looks as though the younger child cannot retain his unique experiences (presumably because he has not yet built up meaningful schemata into which to fit them) and this is a major factor in 'infantile amnesia'. We cannot recollect our very early experiences because they left no adequate impression to begin with.

The quantitative facts of early memories can, then, be explained by the combined effects of retroactive interference and of poor initial learning ability. But what of the qualitative findings? How can we account for the recollecting of this or that particular experience and for the predominance of pleasant and neutral memories? As regards explaining why certain, sometimes apparently trivial, experiences should be readily recalled while others are not, present-day psychology is at a loss. Apart from suggesting that the recollected experiences must, in some way, have been important for the child, no satisfactory explanation has yet been offered. As regards the disproportionately small number of unpleasant memories, a simple explanation would exist if it could be shown that, in the child's life, there were, in fact, more pleasant and neutral experiences than unpleasant ones. And there are one or two pieces of evidence which indicate strongly that this is the case.

Thus, it has been found that smiling and laughing are displayed considerably more frequently in normal children of pre-school age than is crying as a symptom of anger or grief. To the extent that such outward signs may be trusted, it would appear that pleasant and neutral tones predominate greatly over unpleasant states in normal children. The conclusion seems clear that the proportion of pleasant to unpleasant memories may well reflect directly the proportion of originally pleasant and unpleasant experience. In addition to this, there is the effect which different amounts of rehearsal have on the retaining of past experiences. In our conversation and probably also in our private reveries, we tend to recall (and so rehearse) our pleasant experiences and avoid the unpleasant, just as we tend to use pleasant or neutral words in speech and neglect unpleasant words. The tendency of children to avoid words with unpleasant connotations was shown impressively by one psychologist, who made an analysis of the remarks of children aged between five and nine years and found that the ratio of pleasant to unpleasant words was no less than 1,057 to 80. If we do indeed, as seems likely, recall (and so keep alive) our pleasant experiences more often than our unpleasant ones, this would further increase the preponderance of pleasant memories in a way which is selective but has nothing to do with repression. The unpleasant is not actively inhibited but merely loses out in competition with the pleasant. And, of course, an experience which was originally disagreeable may, in being recounted to others, lose its unpleasant tone and even seem pleasant on recall as, for example, when we laugh about our discomfitures in a previously embarrassing situation.

In conclusion of this section on the recollecting of childhood experiences, explanations exist both in terms of repression and also in more conventional terms. The writer would prefer to accept the latter type of explanation as being more consistent with general findings in the field of memory and with the facts of childhood memory as outlined in Chapter One. But it should be realized that there is no specific evidence against Freud's explanation. Present knowledge is not such that we can easily decide between the alternative theories. Even our conventional explanation is not altogether satisfactory in that it contains too many untested assumptions. In this respect, it reflects the present condition of psychology itself, which contains too few facts and too many question marks.

5. THE MEMORY ACCENTUATION EFFECT

At this point, it may not be inappropriate to leave the topic of repressing and discuss a further phenomenon of childhood memory which seems to be familiar to a great many people. It may be called the 'memory accentuation effect', since its chief characteristic is that we recollect the particular object as being larger than it now appears. On seeing again some object (a house, room, street, bridge, toy) which we have not directly perceived since childhood, it often appears as strikingly smaller and less impressive than our recollecting of it. The following personal experience of the writer may be given as an example.

I was motoring through a town which I had last visited twenty-three years before at the age of four. On that previous occasion, I had been taken through a certain school in this town by a relative who was a teacher there. And on several occasions since, I had vividly recollected this tour of inspection, largely in terms of visual imagery. I had recalled the large cement-covered playground in front of the school, the high iron railings, the grey stone façade of the building itself, the class-room on the left of the vast main doorway, and the enormous gymnasium at the end of the lengthy corridor. I still recall being impressed, as a child, with the vastness of the whole building. On seeing the school again, it seemed to have shrunk to such an alarming extent that I had to be reassured by someone else that this was, in fact, the same school. The railings were small, the playground tiny, and the building itself, although moderately sized, diminutive compared with my recollection of it.

Now, it has been pointed out in the previous chapter that there is nothing passive or impersonal about the way in which we perceive the world around us. We perceive events in accordance with our own accumulated past experiences and present needs, that is, we assimilate them to our schemata. We find a book interesting or dull; we see a face as handsome or plain. And we do so because, whether we are aware of it or not, we are relating the present experience to some schema (some subjective yardstick, frame of reference, or body of knowledge) which we have acquired in the course of our daily living. In reading a large number of books, we have built up a body of implicit knowledge about books in terms of which we rate the present book as good or bad. We have seen a great many faces and built up a frame of reference in relation to which we perceive any present face in the way we do. It was also pointed out that these schemata are not static but change as we widen our range of past experiences and develop new needs. This means that our perceiving also varies and that the same event which, at one time, is perceived as interesting or beautiful may, at some later time, be seen as dull or plain. Normally, we are not aware that our modes of perceiving have undergone and are undergoing change, since the transformations are gradual. But most of us will agree that, on reflection, we have altered our way of experiencing things, at least in regard to what we call 'taste'. We are, most of us, aware that our notions of what is pleasing in art and literature have changed and that a book which we once found good may now be regarded by us as bad or mediocre. The same is true not only of 'taste' but of all our perceiving. In recent years, several psychologists have demonstrated the truth of this under laboratory conditions. The way in which a subject perceives any object can be experimentally varied by selectively increasing his range of experiences with similar objects in one direction rather than another. It is possible, for example, to have a subject lift a certain series of weights and so change his judgement of one particular weight from 'heavy' to 'light' and back to 'heavy' again without his being in the least aware of any change in his own perceiving. The important point simply is that our schemata change with new experiences and therefore so does our perceiving. The same object which was formerly perceived as large, or heavy, or beautiful may now be perceived as small, or light, or plain, depending on how our schemata have been moulded by our intervening experiences.

It follows that we may recollect with reasonable accuracy our experience of an object and yet this recollecting of it may be at odds with our present perceiving of the same object. There is disparity between something as recalled and that same thing as experienced in the present. But it may not be the object itself which has changed, or even our recollecting of our original experience of it. Rather, it may be the way in which we perceive it which has altered.

To return to the writer's experience on revisiting the school after twenty-three years, there are two ways in which, between childhood and adulthood, a person's perceiving of the size of a building may change. First, the building may appear larger to the child than to the adult because the child is himself physically smaller. The corridor appears longer because he has to take more steps in traversing it, and it appears higher because he must tilt his head more sharply in order to view the roof which seems as high as the sky. The doors are heavier because he must push harder to open them. The door handles are higher because he must reach up to them, and they are larger because he cannot close his fingers around them. The railings are higher because they tower above his head whereas they only reach the adult's shoulder. Second, the building may appear larger to the child because of the contrast between it and the buildings to which he is accustomed. He has probably had less acquaintance with large buildings, class rooms, halls, and long corridors than the adult has had. His frame of reference for buildings is likely to have been acquired in terms of his own home and the houses of friends rather than in terms of the larger spaces of public buildings such as schools, theatres, museums, hospitals, and the like. In visiting a school at the age of four, the writer was probably coming into intimate contact for the first time with a building which was more commodious than a domestic dwelling house, so that, as compared with his past experiences, the school would appear truly enormous. Being impressed by the school's vast proportions is, indeed, the most vivid aspect of his recollected experience, and it seems likely that it was this impressiveness which made the experience as 'memorable' as it is. In short, the same building may look larger to the child than to the adult because of the former's physical size and also (in the special case of large public buildings) because of the more restricted circumstances under which he has acquired his frame of reference for buildings.

In later years, the individual may reinstate his early experience of the building as relative to his size at that early time. If he does not see this building again for some years, he will now experience it as relative to his present size and, as compared with his recollecting of his original experience, the building will seem to have shrunk. It is not so much that his experience, as recollected, is distorted as that it is accurate relative to a frame of reference which now no longer exists since his schemata have been remoulded by the accumulated effects of intervening experience. Other buildings with which he comes into daily contact do not appear to shrink in this way for the reason that his perceiving of them changes so gradually that the change is not noticed. And in so far as he recollects specific past experiences of these buildings, these too will undergo continual modification as a consequence of frequent retroactive interference. There is, incidentally, no suggestion that such altered perceiving is the only factor contributing to the 'accentuation effect'. There may also be a concomitant change in actual recollecting. If the size were a dominant characteristic of the original experience, this characteristic may well, as has already been noted, become sharpened and even more dominant in intervening recall. Such a qualitative sharpening in recalling presumably occurs in those instances where the object which appears to have shrunk is one which was perceived for the first time during adult life.

In summary of this chapter, we have seen that certain mentally ill people manifest a process of actively and unconsciously inhibiting their recall of painful experiences. The results of psycho-analytic therapy suggest that, like so many processes which are most evident under abnormal conditions, this process also occurs in all normal people with the adaptive consequence of lessening anxiety. It may also be operative in some few instances of 'lapse of memory', but there seem to be no good grounds for assuming that it plays any major role in either temporary forgetting or our inability to recollect our early childhood experiences.

CHAPTER SIX

IMAGING

I

THE 'mind's eye' is a phrase the meaning of which, to almost everyone except the congenitally blind, is readily understood in terms of our personal experience. It is in the 'mind's eye' that we see the face of an absent friend or, like Wordsworth, a host of dancing daffodils. And we say that we have an image of the friend or of the flowers. But although the word 'image' is obviously derived from the realm of seeing, it is used not only in regard to seeing but also in regard to hearing, tasting, smelling, touching, the experiences of temperature, of bodily conditions, of muscular movement, and of strain. It is used, in short, to refer to all instances in which we reinstate some past perceptual experience regardless of the nature of the experience. In the quiet of our home, we may, as it were, relive some past and complex experience. Not only may we see again the high green hills, the blue sky, and the light-flecked waves breaking against the rocky shore, but we may also hear again the cries of the sea-birds and the sound of the ship's hooter. We may smell again the odour of the wrack on the shore and the perfume of the rose in our lapel. We may taste the chocolate we ate on that day, and feel again the warmth of the sun on our face, our movements in walking along the heaving deck, and the sinking experience of oncoming sea-sickness. In all such cases, we are recalling our past experiences in terms of imagery. We know from our personal experience that such imagery may be a conspicuous characteristic of our own recalling, and many of us would agree with Wordsworth that our 'inward eye' – or ear, or nose, etc. – is 'the bliss of solitude'. Many of us derive great pleasure from these various images of our past experiences and from combining them 'in imagination' to produce new and exciting experiences which have no direct counterpart in our perceiving, either past or present. It is to a discussion of this imaging aspect of recall that the present chapter is devoted.

The psychological study of imaging has had a curious history over the past half-century. Following the pioneer work of Sir Francis Galton, there was lively interest in the topic. Then starting in about the twenties, progressively less attention was paid to imaging until, today, it is a process more discussed by novelists and literary men than by psychologists. The reason for this strange course of events is really very simple. The great advances of psychology in the present century have been due to the adoption of the scientific method. The discoveries which have been and continue with increasing momentum to be made about psychological processes have resulted from a gradually evolving methodology, an increase in techniques of observation and experiment. The students of man himself have, like the students of physics and of biology before them, discovered by devising ever more ingenious and precise methods of observing the phenomena in question. But the study of imaging, and of the contents of conscious awareness in general, have not shared the fruits of this methodological progress. A number of techniques have been tried out but, again and again, psychologists have failed to discover any new way of investigating the contents of conscious experience. They have simply had to fall back on the verbal descriptions which people give of their imaging. As yet, there is nothing for it but to accept people's word that their imaging is what they say it is, and we are in no position to check the accuracy or otherwise of their statements. If two individuals say that they have a 'vivid' image, how do we know that they are each using the word 'vivid' in exactly the same way ? If someone gives but a fragmentary account of his imaging, how do we know that it is his imaging and not his describing which is sketchy ? If someone gives a highly elaborate account of his imaging, how do we know that he is not deceiving us – and himself – by his description, that he is not reporting as being simultaneously present features which are actually successive, that he is not being forced by the mould of language into giving a grossly distorted account of what he sees ? The answer to all these doubts is that we do not know, and perhaps we never shall. The descriptions which people give of their imaging are interesting and, up to a point, instructive. But once we have collected examples of these descriptions, we can go little further. Psychologists have stopped making substantial contributions to the study of imaging for the simple reason that, in the absence of objective methods for its observation, there are few if any new contributions to be made. Discussions of a speculative nature have, of course, continued and there has recently been hope that the developing techniques of recording the electrical activity of the brain (electroencephalography) may cast light on the nature and function of imaging. However, these new electrical methods hold out, as yet, no more than a promise and, meanwhile, our knowledge of imaging advances but little. It is scarcely surprising, therefore, that this book on memory should allot so much space to recalling as it occurs in terms of words, drawings, and other objectively observable performances and so little space to the more intimate, but exclusively personal, recall in terms of imaging.

The discouraging tenor of the above discussion should not be allowed to obscure the fact that what people have to say about their imaging has given rise to a number of interesting findings worthy of mention. But before proceeding to give account of these findings, it might be as well to distinguish the memory image from the related phenomena of the negative and positive after-image. Incidentally, this use of the noun 'image' must not lead us to assume that there is any such entity as *the* image. Strictly speaking, we ought to talk not of the image of a scene but rather of imaging the scene or of experiencing the scene in the absence of any appropriate external stimulation such as exists in perceiving. In the interests of easy expression, we may talk of images as things instead of as processes provided we always bear in mind that such language is more metaphorical than precise.

2. NEGATIVE AND POSITIVE AFTER-IMAGES

The reader who has not experienced a negative after-image for himself might care to try the following little experiment. Take as the stimulus a scrap of brightly coloured paper about, say, the size of a penny and make a tiny pencil mark or pin-prick near its centre. Lay this on a sheet of white paper and look fixedly at the mark in its centre for perhaps twenty seconds. Remove the coloured stimulus and fixate with the eyes some tiny mark on the large white sheet. After a few seconds during which nothing may happen, a patch of colour will be seen. If we continue fixating, this patch will vanish, then return only to vanish once more; it may alternately appear and disappear as many as twenty or thirty times, growing fainter with each successive reappearance until a time is reached after a minute or so when it disappears altogether. Now, there are two surprising things about this image. The first is its colour. If the stimulus is red, the image is green; if the stimulus is blue, the image is yellow; if the stimulus is black, the image is white. The image has, in short, that colour which is described as being complementary to the colour of the stimulus, and it is for this reason that the after-image is called 'negative'. If, after fixating the stimulus, we fixate not the white sheet but some coloured surface, the image changes colour accordingly. Suppose the stimulus had been green. On a white or grey surface, the image is red; on a yellow surface, the image is orange; on a blue surface, the image is purple; on a green surface (the same colour as the stimulus), the image is grey and colourless; and on a red surface, the image is a highly saturated red of great brilliance. The second surprising thing about the negative after-image is its size. Suppose a 1-inch square stimulus is fixated at a distance of 1 foot from the eye. If the after-image is then obtained by fixating a surface which is also 1 foot away, the image will cover exactly 1 square inch of this surface. But if this surface is 2, 5, 10, or 15 feet distant from the eye, the image will be 2, 5, 10, or 15 inches in diameter. Thus, the size of the image varies with the distance between the observer and the surface on which he projects the image. In fact, the size of the image is directly proportional to the distance of the projection surface from the eye. This generalization is known as Emmert's Law, and we will have occasion to refer back to it later in the chapter.

The reader can fairly readily obtain all the above-mentioned effects for himself, although a little trial and error may be necessary to establish the most favourable conditions. The clearness and duration of the negative after-image depend on such factors as the colour and brilliance of the stimulus, the background on which it lies, the conditions of illumination, and the length and accuracy of fixation. The image is clearer the simpler the stimulus; complicated stimuli, such as a detailed picture, give either a very poor image or none at all. These effects are all readily understandable in terms of the psycho-physical properties of light but, in this book, there is neither the space nor the necessity to give an account of these properties. The interested reader will find a description of them in any of the standard introductory text-books of psychology. Here, it suffices merely to say that the effects are due to the adaptation or 'fatigue' of the colour- and light-sensitive tissue (the retina) which lies at the back of the eyeball. In fixating the red stimulus patch, we continuously stimulate the same area of the retina until it becomes no longer sensitive to the red of the patch. (As we fixate the stimulus, we may notice that it seems to lose its colour except round the edges.) Then when we fixate some other surface, this adapted retinal area is insensitive to whatever red component the surface possesses and the negative after-image results. As we continue to fixate, the retina adapts to the colour of the new surface and the image wanes. The important point is that the image is the after-effect of continuously stimulating and so 'fatiguing' a specific area of the retina.

The positive after-image is essentially in the nature of perseveration. Some stimulus is present for a moment and then vanishes, but we continue to experience the effects of the stimulus as though it still persisted. The positive after-image is less easy to demonstrate than is the negative, but we have probably all experienced it at some time or other. We glance at a brightly lit object, then turn our eyes to a dark wall and see 'inwardly' the object still before us and in its original colour. The majority of us have experienced the positive after-image which follows our looking at the sun or a dazzling light. In the realm of hearing, we have had the embarrassing experience of not 'catching' a question, asking for it to be repeated, and then hearing the words 'in the mind's ear' and answering them before our questioner can say the words again.

It is also well known that the strokes of a clock which have not been attended to during the striking may sometimes be counted immediately afterwards and the whole succession of strokes may be repeated in awareness with a vividness almost comparable to an actual perceiving of the sounds at the time. Usually such perseveration is extremely short-lived, but there are circumstances under which it may persist for a considerable time. For example, many people are troubled by experiencing continued movement after a journey by sea or train; and people who are exceptionally sensitive to light often report that a long day's fishing in bright light is followed by positive after-images of the pools and foliage which are so vivid as to interfere with relaxation and reading.

Both the negative and positive after-image resemble the memory image proper in that they exist in the absence of a present, appropriate, external stimulus. But they can be distinguished from the memory image, in relative if not in absolute terms, by the conditions of their appearance. They occur very shortly after the withdrawal of the stimulus, whereas the memory image typically occurs much later and is subject to a distinctly voluntary control not shared by the after-images as such.

3. MEMORY IMAGES

In 1883, Sir Francis Galton published a book entitled *Inquiries into Human Faculty and its Development*. In this work, he reported the outcome of several ingenious investigations into the activities of human beings and made not a few observations which presaged much of later psychological investigation. It is written with the modest and lively simplicity of true greatness and, although some of its conclusions have had to be revised, it remains into the present day a book which well repays the reading of it. Our present interest in Galton's book lies in the account given of the answers to a questionnaire which he sent out to 100 men, at least half of whom were distinguished in science or some other field of intellectual endeavour. In this questionnaire, he asked his respondents to recall their breakfast table as they sat down to it that morning, to consider carefully the pictures which arise in their 'mind's eye', and to answer a list of searching questions about these pictures. They were also asked about the vividness and detail with which they could image experiences to do with hearing, smelling, tasting, touching, and such bodily experiences as cold, hunger, drowsiness, and fever. They were further asked to contribute supplementary information and general remarks as they felt inclined.

When Galton had received the answers and tabulated them, the most outstanding result was the enormous range of differences between one individual and the next. At one extreme, there were individuals who reported imagery as bright and clear as the actually perceived scene. Their images were never blotchy or indistinct, but brilliant and as rich in their particulars as though the breakfast table were, at this moment, in front of them. At the other extreme, there were individuals who could report no imagery at all. They could recollect the table in verbal terms, even as regards colour, but there were no images of it. One artist reported that he could draw a likeness of both people and places some days or weeks after seeing them, but this was the result of having studied the appearances while present and of trial and error sketching at the time of reproduction: no visual imagery was involved. Several individuals reported that their only experience of imagery had occurred in that drowsy state which lies between waking and sleeping. But some individuals had, presumably, not experienced imagery even during this state and could not even understand what was meant by Galton's questions. So deficient were they in imaging that they regarded other people's accounts of their imaging as mere romancing. Such an individual is in the same position regarding images as is a colour-blind man regarding colour—it falls completely outwith his range of awareness.

Since Galton's time, other psychologists have supplemented his findings by asking people questions about their imaging. In order to facilitate comparisons between individuals, the subjects are usually asked to rate each image in terms of a prearranged set of categories such as the following. (I) Perfectly clear and as vivid as the actual experience: (II) Very clear and comparable in vividness to the actual experience: (III) Moderately clear and vivid: (IV) Not clear or vivid but recognizable: (V) Vague and dim: (VI) So vague and dim as to be hardly noticeable: (VII) No image present at all. Once these categories have been explained, subjects are asked to apply them while trying to image a variety of different experiences. They may be asked, for example, to attempt the following. Try to get a visual image of a glove, house, fire burning, sunset: try to get an auditory image of the bark of a dog, beat of rain on a window, click of a teaspoon in a saucer, swish of a silk dress, honk of a motor car: try to get a kinaesthetic image of marching, lifting a heavy weight, running upstairs, saying 'God save the King', nodding your head in assent: try to get a tactile image of velvet, emery-paper, heat of a warm fire, wet soap, cold rain on your face: try to get a gustatory image of salt, orange juice, chocolate, cheese, coffee: try to get an olfactory image of cigar smoke, tar, onions, camphor, roses: try to get an organic image of a headache, fatigue, a sore throat, nausea, repletion after a full meal.

The answers given by people to such questions as the above serve mainly to emphasize the wide range of individual differences noted by Galton. As indicated, imaging may occur in any one of at least seven sensory modes: it may be visual, tactile, and so on. One person may report imaging which is as vivid in any mode as in any other. Another may report poor ability to image in any mode. Yet another may report vivid imaging in one mode or some combination of modes and little or none in the remainder. Differences even occur within a single mode, as, for example, in the ability to obtain coloured imaging. In short, the possible variations both between and within modes are so tremendous that it is impossible to make any simple generalizations about them. Early psychologists hoped that it might be possible to classify people into groups or types according to the characteristics of their imaging. The terms 'visile', 'audile', and 'motile' were coined for those whose imaging was predominantly visual, auditory, and kinaesthetic, respectively. However, although often suggestive, people's reports fail to furnish definite evidence that clear-cut categories can be established.

Despite these enormous, and as yet unclassifiable, differences between individuals, it is possible to draw four conclusions concerning general tendencies. First, visual imaging is the most common and, for most people, is also the most vivid. Auditory imaging is next most frequent, followed by tactile imagery. Kinaesthetic, gustatory, and organic imagery occur next with about the same frequency, while olfactory imaging is the least common and vivid mode of all. Second, people who report being particularly good in one mode of imaging also tend to report being above average in other modes as well. This would seem to indicate that the majority of us are versatile rather than restricted in our modes of imaging. While there are notable individual exceptions, it therefore appears that what imaging ability we have tends to be all-round rather than limited to one or a few sensory modes. Third, imaging occurs with especial frequency and vividness in the hypnagogic state, that is, the state between waking and sleeping. For many people, this state is particularly rich in imagery. Vivid, life-like scenes pass before the 'inner eye' and voices are distinctly heard. Usually such hypnagogic imaging requires no voluntary effort and may even occur despite our attempts to suppress it, the images sometimes appearing to be so real as to approach or attain the character of hallucinations.

The fourth and last – and in some ways the most interesting – general finding has two related aspects. One aspect is that the imaging of the self-same person varies according to what he is trying to recall. If it is a concrete, unique object such as a face or a voice, imaging tends to occur more frequently than if it is an abstract argument, a decision, or a logical deduction. Even although these latter items were originally experienced in concrete terms, such as a seen or heard communication, their recalling is accomplished with a lesser accompaniment of imaging. The second aspect of this fourth conclusion is that people who deal chiefly with abstract lines of thinking report a less than average ability to 'summon up' images. This fact was first noted by Galton who found his hundred men of intellectual distinction lower in imaging ability than children and adults selected from non-professional walks of life. Confirmation came in 1909 from an American psychologist, G. H.

Betts, when he asked both college students and professors about their imaging. The students most frequently reported their imaging as slightly better than 'moderately clear and vivid' while the professors most frequently reported it as slightly better than 'vague and dim'. The relation between skill in abstract thinking and lack of imaging ability seems well established, although it is to be emphasized that it holds only in average terms and that there are, as always, individuals who constitute striking exceptions to the rule. We shall return to this relation again at the end of the chapter but, here, it may be said that the reason for it seems to be that the more efficient and successful the thinking, at least of a logical nature, the less it is accompanied for most people by imaging. It would appear that images are too concrete and specific to be of great service in reaching solutions by high-level thinking. And as the individual's skill in abstract thinking develops, it increasingly interferes with and weakens his somewhat outmoded skill in imaging until he may not be able to image even when specifically asked to do so.

Image-Association. Before leaving this section, one last and curious finding may be mentioned, namely, that of 'image-association'. There are people whose recalling of certain items is consistently accompanied by imaging which has no apparent relation to the items concerned. Thus, individuals manifest what is known as a 'number-form'. This involves imaging a spatial arrangement of numbers and, whenever a number is thought of, it is imaged in this way. The number-form may be a sloping curve with irregularities at the points of important numbers, or it may be a three-dimensional lattice of some sort. The form varies much from individual to individual and is usually complex. But despite its complexity, there is nothing vague about the form and its possessor is confident of being able to construct, say, a wire model of it. These forms are also persistent, remaining largely unchanged throughout the years. (For descriptions and drawings of various number forms, the reader is referred to Galton's book.) Incredible though such forms may seem to those of us who do not experience them ourselves, it is probable that most of us have the undeveloped foundations of one in our own awareness. Thus, one investigator questioned 250 people who claimed to have no number-forms and found that no fewer than 210 reported a feeling that numbers somehow receded from them: some reported that numbers had a vague upward movement and others that they seemed to recede in a straight line or at an angle.

The number-form is not the only example of image-association. Numbers, months of the year, and days of the week are also quite commonly recalled in terms of visual imaging involving either spatial relations or colours or objects. One case reported to the writer involves the vivid visual imaging of objects whenever the days of the week are thought of. This imaging has, to the writer's knowledge, remained substantially unchanged for the past ten years and his informant (whom we may call X) claims to have had just these particular image-associations since as far back as he can recollect. In very brief, the associations are as follows. Monday — a window of a factory where X's father worked when X was a child (and to which he returned on Mondays): Tuesday — a small white handkerchief with 'A Merry Christmas' embroidered in red across one corner: Wednesday — a man's black striped trousers (such as X's father wore to attend a committee which met every Wednesday during X's childhood): Thursday — a light-brown earthenware jar: Friday — an earthenware jar similar to the former but much darker in colour: Saturday — a saucer with a pattern of brown and gold squares round the edge (this was part of the 'good china' which was used on Saturdays because X's father was at home for tea on that day): Sunday — a metal cream pitcher (used only on Sundays when X's family had cream instead of milk for lunch and tea). It seems clear from this sketchy report that at least four of these associations derive from those recurrent events which, for the young child, differentiated one day of the week from another. Unfortunately, the sources of most image-associations are not so evident and are often completely obscure. Why these associations should persist over the years and whether they serve any function are questions which have not yet been answered. To date, the quite normal phenomenon of image-association appears to be in the nature of a psychological curiosity.

4. PHOTOGRAPHIC MEMORY

From time to time we hear people refer to 'photographic memory' and say wistfully how useful the gift must be. By this term is meant, presumably, the ability to image an absent scene with all the vividness, distinctness, and detail of a photographic print. Since many people suppose such an ability to exist, this section is devoted to an examination of the evidence for such a supposition. What approximates most closely to the popular notion of 'photographic memory' is a remarkable form of visual imaging which has been estimated to occur in something like 1 to 10 per cent of the adult population and 50 to 60 per cent of children under the age of 12 years. This form of imaging was first investigated by the German psychologist, E. R. Jaensch, and found to have so many unique characteristics that it was given the name 'eidetic' (virtually, identical or duplicative).

The observations of Jaensch and others on eidetic imaging have been summarized by G. W. Allport in an article published in 1924 in the *British Journal of Psychology*. Allport himself worked in Cambridge with some sixty 11-year-old children, and his procedure may be mentioned because it is typical. At a normal reading distance from the child, he propped up a 2-foot square dark grey mat on which he placed, one at a time, pictures cut from an ordinary picture book. The pictures were rich in detail and action, the principal features being in silhouette and the background objects coloured in delicate tints. A picture was left on the mat for thirty-five seconds, during which time the child scrutinized it carefully. It was then removed and the child was simply asked to look at the grey mat and report what he saw. Thirty of the children then behaved in a most striking manner. It was as though they were still actually seeing the picture. Their imaging was unusually vivid and contained details of the absent picture with an almost photographic fidelity. This is eidetic imaging, and it differs from the more usual form of imaging in a number of respects, the chief of which concern its localization, its intensity, and its richness of detail.

As regards localization, the eidetic image is seen as situated in outer space. It is never localized 'within the head', as the usual memory image so often is, but 'out there', attached to the mat or a wall or some other surface. It is as though the child were looking at a picture on this surface and, indeed, if the surface is folded or bent then the 'picture' too is likewise folded or bent. However, despite this 'outer' character of the image, the subject always recognizes that it is a purely subjective phenomenon, that it is an effect which he is voluntarily producing, and that it has no outer, objective existence. As regards vividness, the image is so clear and strong that it tends to obscure the background against which it is projected. In this respect again, it is as though there were a filmy but almost opaque picture on the projection surface. In always appearing as projected on a surface in outer space, the eidetic image closely resembles the negative after-image. However, the two phenomena are by no means identical. For one thing, the negative after-image occurs only after the prolonged fixation of a relatively simple object, whereas the eidetic image occurs after the very different activity of letting the eyes rove hither and thither over an object rich in complex detail. For another thing, the eidetic image differs from both the positive and negative after-image in being more persistent: not only does it last longer, but it can be voluntarily revived some hours, weeks, or even months later. A further difference is that the eidetic image does not, like the negative after-image, vary its size with the distance between the subject and the projection surface: it does not obey Emmert's Law, for, while undergoing some slight change in size with distance, it is roughly constant for positions of the projection surface, at least between 25 and 100 cm. A final difference between the eidetic and the after-image is that, as we shall shortly see, the former is subject to qualitative distortions of a kind which never occur in the latter.

The most striking characteristic of the eidetic image is the wealth of detail it contains. Details are reported from the image such as the number of buttons on the jacket of a passer-by, the length and direction of the lines of shading in a stretch of roadway, and the number of whiskers on a cat's lip. The individual appears to be able to focus upon any detail and make it become gradually clearer so that the rest of the 'picture' becomes obscure. It is this richness of detail which sets the eidetic image apart from the usual memory image, and this difference between the two can be demonstrated directly. When, after the picture is removed, the children are not asked to look at the grey mat but are asked merely to describe the picture, they do this without recourse to eidetic imaging. If they are then asked to turn their eyes to the grey mat, they supplement their account with what they 'see' there. Allport found that, with scarcely a single exception, the eidetic imaging supplied detail lacking in conventional recalling, and it sometimes happened that a child, on the evidence of his eidetic image, would spontaneously correct a misstatement which he had made in his previous account 'from memory'. We may give just one example of the amazing details which may be 'read off' the image. One of the pictures used by Allport depicted a street scene and contained, among other details, the German word *Gartenwirthschaft* written above the door of an inn in the background. This word was quite meaningless for the English children and was not usually reported at first, the subjects starting with descriptions of the more outstanding and dramatic features of the image. But on being pressed to observe more closely, each of the thirty children whose eidetic imaging was strong saw, often to his surprise, the small letters above the door. Three of these children spelled out the word without error, seven got no more than two of the letters wrong, and only five failed to give at least five letters correctly. In all cases, the letters were given with equal accuracy whether 'read off' from left to right or in the reverse order. There was, of course, no question of the word having been memorized. The exposure of thirty-five seconds was insufficient for this, especially since the picture itself was filled with incident and details of lively interest which the child was likewise able to describe from his imaging.

From what has been said, it might well be supposed that eidetic imaging is photographic in its accuracy. Such, however, is not the case. The child cannot see each and every detail of the original, as witness the fact that the majority of Allport's 'eidetic children' were unable to 'read off' every letter in the long German word. Thus, the imaging, although truly remarkable in its detail, is not to be compared with a photographic reproducing of the original. Those parts of the picture which proved most interesting are likely to be seen in the image, while the less interesting parts tend to be either faint or absent altogether. For example, one investigator found that, of a group of children who gave a vivid eidetic image of a picture depicting a monkey, half failed to image an uninteresting picture of an ordinary house. In addition to the tendency to omit uninteresting details, there are also qualitative distortions. The child may change the position or character of some of the details or even add an item entirely lacking in the original. These distortions and added details are also vividly seen in the image and there is nothing to distinguish them as innovations. Such changes are especially frequent when the picture is imaged after a considerable lapse of time. But this is not all. Many pictures portraying action result in an image where the action is carried to completion. On occasion, this movement in the image is voluntarily produced: a carriage is made to drive away, turn a corner in the road, and so disappear altogether from the image; people are made to enter and leave the 'scene' and perform various normal actions. Sometimes this movement may also be produced at the suggestion of the experimenter. In an investigation reported in 1926 by the American psychologist H. Kluver, both voluntary and spontaneous movements appeared in the eidetic images of animal pictures. In imaging a picture containing a donkey standing some distance from a manger, the donkey crossed over to the manger, moved his ears, bent his neck, and began to eat. Suggestions from Kluver to the effect that the donkey was hungry sometimes served to set in motion a series of changes which surprised the imaging subjects themselves. It was as if they were not now looking at a static picture but at a living scene, for, as soon as the suggestion was given, the donkey would 'spontaneously' race over to the manger. It is noteworthy that all these distortions, additions, and movements which occur in eidetic imaging are, like the qualitative changes which occur in recalling generally, in full accordance with the

subject's framework of expectations. They are always consistent with the child's normal experiences and he is definitely
unable to introduce into his imaging features which are
ridiculous or unnatural.

Thus, for all its rich detail, eidetic imaging is neither
literally reproductive nor static, and the larger the interval
between the original seeing and the imaging, the greater the
likelihood of distortion and change. Even in the eidetic image –
the nearest approximation which psychology has found to
'photographic memory' – there are additions, omissions, and
distortions and, as in recalling generally, the role of selective
interests and accumulated past experiences is evident. The
same is true of eidetic imaging in adults. Some remarkable
examples of this have been recorded but, wherever these have
been adequately investigated, it has been found that the
imaging is far from being photographic. We may here cite only
one investigation, that reported by W. A. Bousfield and H.
Barry in the *American Journal of Psychology* in 1933. The
subject of their study was Mr Salo Finkelstein, a Polish
calculating genius who must be placed among the world's
foremost calculators. He was hired by an American broadcasting company to tally returns of the 1932 Presidential
election because, it was stated, he was faster than any
calculating machine. Shortly after the election, he allowed himself to be experimented upon in various ways by Bousfield and
Barry, and the results of these experiments revealed the truly
amazing quality of his genius which concerned, first, his extraordinary speed in the mental manipulation of figures and,
second, his vivid visual imaging. It is this second characteristic
which is of interest here, and we could do no better than quote
what Bousfield and Barry have to say concerning it.

In respect to the question of visual imagery, it is evident that
the imaginal process is virtually integrated into the processes of
memorization and calculation, and without it the involved
manipulations of figures would undoubtedly be impossible. The
imagery may be said to serve a reference function, since numbers resulting from various calculations and numbers which have
acquired significance through associations are chalked down,
so to speak, and held in readiness for subsequent reference.

The imagery, accordingly, leaves the attention free for subsequent calculations, and there is no necessity for continuous
review of the figures in order that retention may take place.
Certain of the more prominent features of this imagery for
numbers are as follows: (a) The numbers appear as if written
with chalk on a freshly washed blackboard. (b) The numbers
are in Mr Finkelstein's own handwriting regardless of the form
of presentation. (c) Ordinarily the numbers appear to be from
5 to 7 cm. in height. (d) The images normally appear to be at a
distance of 35 to 40 cm. from the eyes. (e) The span of imagery
includes about six figures with a definite preference for their
horizontal arrangement. If, for example, a list of 200 numbers
has been memorized, at any one moment any group of about six
figures may be made to stand out clearly. (f) When the figures
are visualized on a ground at a distance of about $1\frac{1}{2}$ m., they are
about 30 per cent smaller and less distinct. Emmert's law of the
proportionate variation of the size of the after-image with the
distance of the projection ground from the eye seems to be
reversed.

Notice that in this, perhaps the most amazing case of adult
eidetic imaging yet investigated, the imaging is, again, not
photographic. The numbers always appear in Mr Finkelstein's
own handwriting. Furthermore, his ability to image depends
on his interest in the material as shown by his imaging letters
of the alphabet as being both smaller in size and less distinct
than his images of numbers. (His inability to image the colour
of numbers originally presented in colour was found to be
partly, but not entirely, due to an actual defect in his colour
vision.) There are also instances of errors in his imaging. He
can voluntarily and accurately image a square of digits, composed of five rows of five digits each, shown to him two hours
before. But his imaging is not always accurate, for there are
definite indications of retroactive interference, errors occasionally being introduced in the imaging as a result of having
memorized a subsequent list. Thus, in all these respects, his
imaging departs markedly from a photograph of the original.
Nor is his memorizing at the time of original presentation
accomplished through the passive ease of clicking any mental
camera shutter. It is a process which requires deliberate and
fully conscious handling of the figures and the active relating

of them to number sequences and combinations already made familiar by past experiences.

Does there, then, exist anything to correspond with the popular notion of 'photographic memory'? From what has been said, the answer is clearly in the negative. Remarkable though eidetic imaging may be, it in no wise suggests the static, duplicative characteristics of a photograph. It resembles any other instance of recalling in being a constructive process and it manifests the same forms of distortion which have already been seen to be typical of such constructing. Exactly how this re-constructing of the past is achieved is the chief mystery of memory. It is a mystery which psychology has failed to dispel. Perhaps it is a mystery which will never yield up its secrets to the methods of empirical scientific investigation. But the fact that it is a re-constructing rather than a literal reproducing points up a principle which seems to have universal application (a principle which is eloquently elaborated by Sir Frederic Bartlett in his book *Remembering*). Nowhere, in either human or animal activity, do we ever find the individual doing or experiencing exactly the same thing twice. He often does the same sort of thing, but he never literally duplicates any single activity, whether it be a performance or a conscious experience. The steps of a dance, the recital of a poem, the stroke of a tennis match – if these are closely observed there is little difficulty in detecting differences between the 'same' performance as executed to-day and at some other time. The same is true of recalling: it never literally reinstates a past experience or activity. And indeed there seems to be no biologically sound reason why it should. The constantly changing world around us demands that we interact with it in an ever-changing way, and to react to the events of to-day strictly in terms of the performances and experiences of yesterday would be inappropriate. The utility of memory for living lies not in facilitating the operation of the past as it operated before, but rather in facilitating the operation of the past in relation to the somewhat changed conditions of the present. Memory seems to have been evolved to deal only incidentally with those rare situations where we are required to give a flawlessly accurate account of the past. Its primary function is not to conserve the past but to make possible adjustment to the requirements of the present.

Before leaving eidetic imaging, one last characteristic of it deserves mention, namely, its decline with age. It is found that the proportion of people showing eidetic imaging decreases sharply after the age of about eleven years – an age, incidentally, which marks a critical turning-point in the intellectual life of the individual, for it is at this age, on the average, that what we call 'logical' thinking finally emerges. The reason for this decline is not clearly understood, but a large contributing factor seems to be that, with the development of logical thinking, the eidetic image ceases to serve any very useful function for the majority of people. The function of eidetic imaging for the young child has been well expressed by Allport in his 1924 article as follows.

The eidetic image seems to serve essentially the same purpose in the mental development of the child as does the repetition of a stimulus situation. It permits the concrete 'sensory' aspects of the surrounding world to penetrate thoroughly into his mind. The young child delights in conjuring up his images: a parade of soldiers, a circus, a train journey, or even a trivial domestic scene may haunt him for days or weeks, furnishing him material of great interest for his play activities. It is sometimes only with difficulty that he is persuaded to distrust the reality of these vivid images. He reacts to them with the same degree of seriousness as to a genuine stimulus situation: he is terrified by his image of a wild animal; he is contented for hours with the companionship of his imaginary playmate; and he insists dogmatically upon the reality of his most fanciful visions. Such pseudo-sensory experience enables him to 'study out' in his own way and in his own time the various possibilities for response contained within the stimulus situation. His reaction when the situation is first presented is often incomplete, the presence of adults, or the lack of time, preventing him from becoming thoroughly acquainted with its properties. A period of reflection is necessary, during which he may experiment in various ways with his image, varying his behaviour to conform sometimes to one and sometimes to another aspect of the situation, gradually gaining a comprehension of the full meaning of the whole, and building up the attitude which is to determine his future response to the same or to analagous situations.

When he has reached adolescence, the individual's adjustment to the concrete aspects of his environment are reasonably well established, and he now turns from the conquest of the tangible world to the conquest of abstract thinking and personal emotional experiences. In this conquest and in the changing behaviour organization which emerges from it, there is little need for imaging of the eidetic sort. Individuals for whom imaging continues to be especially useful appear to be those who pursue literary or artistic vocations or who are required to manipulate, on a practical level, complex spatial relationships as in architecture or in surgery. But even in these individuals, eidetic imaging would be clearly anomalous. Its function is performed only in the earlier years of mental development and eidetic imaging must now be kept strictly in check if it is not to become a serious liability.

CHAPTER SEVEN

IMPROVING MEMORY

I

AT this stage in the book, the reader will doubtless be in a position to appreciate that the question of improving memory is, as it stands, so broad as to be unanswerable. Memory, as we have seen, is not a faculty, but merely a name used to designate collectively a wide and somewhat heterogeneous range of processes. The chief of these processes are learning, retaining, and remembering. Thus, the question of improving memory breaks down, as a first approximation, into three questions. First, can learning be improved? Second, can retaining be improved? Third, can remembering be improved? The answer to the first of these questions is affirmative. The answer to the second and third is almost certainly negative. Retaining is a physiological process about which little or nothing is known as yet. But at no time in the history of psychological investigation has there been the slightest evidence to suggest that its improvement could be brought about either by training or by any other means. Remembering, as the active process of reconstructing past events out of their retained effects, ought to be susceptible to improvement through practice – at least in theory. But so far, no psychologist has been able to obtain any evidence for the trainability of remembering or to suggest how the activity might be trained. We cannot know what future research may reveal but, for the present, it is safe to say that remembering, as an activity, has hitherto shown itself intractable to deliberately contrived improvement. All this being so, the question of how we can improve our memory reduces, in effect, to the question of how we can learn to learn better. As that great American psychologist, William James, said nearly seventy years ago: all improvement in memory consists in the improvement of one's habitual methods of recording facts.

Now the above conclusion is, in itself, of considerable practical importance. It means that if some occurrence passes without leaving any effect on us, there is absolutely nothing we can do about trying to remember it. The most important step in ensuring that something will be remembered later is to make sure that we learn it at the time. Many of us flaunt this fact in our everyday lives. For example, we are introduced to a stranger and bestow on him but a casual glance; we are told his name and, as often as not, we do not even hear it properly – it is just a mumble against the diffuse background of noise and distraction. And then, almost as though we might expect otherwise, we complain that we cannot remember either the stranger's appearance or his name and excuse ourselves in the socially acceptable manner of shifting the blame to our 'bad memory'. If the reader observes the behaviour of others, and especially of himself, in the social situation of 'introductions', he will be surprised to find how often the above sequence of events takes place. The stranger's name is not remembered for the very simple reason that no effort was made to learn it in the first instance or even perhaps to hear it clearly. We have already seen, in Chapter Two, how valuable it is in memorizing to have an intention to learn. And this is true for the learning of any material, whether it be poems, nonsense syllables, people's names, or appointments. The first essential is to realize that the material presents us with a learning challenge and that this challenge can rarely be met in the absence of a voluntary effort on our part. If the writer were to resort to the hazardous business of laying down rules for the improvement of learning, his first rule would be: Have an intention to learn.

Merely intending to learn is not, however, enough. We are all familiar with having been determined to master some learning task and having failed because, as we say, we do not know how to set about it. We lack what might be called efficient techniques of study. What are these techniques and how can they be acquired? This is the central question of memory improvement, and the remainder of this chapter will be devoted to it. We may, at this point, anticipate further discussion by saying that these techniques are, broadly speaking, three in number. The first is a technique of selective observing or perceiving. The second, and most vital, is a technique of organizing the material to be learned. The third is a technique of distributing the effort of study. This last technique has already been discussed at some length in Chapter Two and little more need be said about it here. It is not a technique which is acquired through any specific training programme. Indeed, it is not a technique which need be acquired except by senior school pupils, university students, public speakers, and others who must learn (on their own) and recall large quantities of material such as most of us are not required to handle in our daily living. If such students are aware of the variables involved – that is, of the relative advantages of spaced practice, study by wholes, and recitation – they acquire, in the pursuit of their studies, a knowledge of that particular combination of distributed efforts which best suits their own unique abilities and learning requirements. There is, however, one principle of effort distribution which has universal application to all learning, whatever its nature. This is the enormous advantage accruing to later remembering through frequent repetition. After initial learning has occurred, its permanence can be ensured by reviewing the material from time to time at intervals so spaced as to allow no serious forgetting to occur between successive repetitions.

What will now be done is to examine, in turn, those training procedures which have been suggested at different times for the improvement of learning and show that, where they succeed, it is because they foster the three study techniques of selective observation, of organization, and of repetition. Over the centuries, many such training procedures have been offered, or sold, to the public at large but, despite their variation in detail, they fall into two broad categories. The first and more straightforward involves practice in memorizing some sort of material. The second and more elaborate involves the acquisition of a set of rules known as a 'mnemonic system'. These systems merit a brief word of introduction.

Into the present day, so-called memory experts have packed halls with audiences eager to witness their feats of memory. These experts are of two kinds. There is the 'memory-man' who specializes in answering factual questions relating to some fairly circumscribed field such as historical dates or sport. He owes his talent to a vast store of knowledge which has been built up over the years not by supernormal means or by the use of mnemonic systems but by the prolonged study of some subject in which, for some reason or other, he is profoundly interested. It is noteworthy that the memory-man facing his audience is comparable to the well-prepared university student taking his final examination and that he may actually be inferior to the latter in the range and spontaneity of his answers. This is not to belittle either the memory-man or the student, but merely to emphasize that the memory-man is someone who can readily recall from an extensive and well-organized body of past learning. As such, he is not so rare as might be imagined. There are many professional and business men and 'enthusiasts' of various sorts who, allowed their own field of specialization and appropriate conditions of publicity and theatricality, could emulate the professional memory-man and not suffer in comparison. The second form of memory expert specializes in memorizing, on the spot, lists of new and un-related material presented to him by his audience. These are the 'mnemonists', and it is they who have evolved and practised mnemonic systems. They do not stop at laying down general principles for memorizing but elaborate highly specific rules. The efficacy of these rules is attested by the mnemonist's amazing performance, for he can memorize, at a single hearing, a series of objects or numbers which, without his system, he would require to study for some considerable time. Whether such systems are of use in everyday life is quite another matter and will be considered later.

Before we pass to a consideration of the training procedures which have been proposed for the improvement of learning, one point should perhaps be made clear. It is that the extent to which any individual can improve his learning abilities is limited by his inherited intellectual capacities. However long or strenuously we try, few of us will ever rival the learning performances of that small section of mankind which is endowed by heredity with a far greater than usual capacity for rapid and efficient learning. In the field of scholarship, Lord Macaulay, the historian, was such a man. He is said to have been able to recall verbatim pages and pages of hundreds of books as a result of having read them only once. In the field of reporting, 'Memory' Woodfall was another such. In the days when newspaper men were forbidden to take notes of speeches made in the British Parliament, he sat in the gallery, placed his elbows on his knees and his head between his hands, and memorized the speeches so that he could later write them out for the Press. The accomplishments of such men were not the fruits of practice alone but also of inherited learning potentialities such as few of us possess. But although our learning capacities seem in some way to be fixed by our genetic history, there are probably none of us who use these capacities as well as we might, who show no room for improvement. To draw a crude analogy, our learning capacities are like a suitcase. The size of the case may be limited but we can pack more by packing more systematically. So, too, our learning capacities may be limited but we can learn more by learning more systematically.

2. PRACTICE IN MEMORIZING

People have been heard to remark that they owe their poor memory to never having been made to learn poetry at school. Such a remark exemplifies, in extreme form, the widespread belief that we can improve our learning abilities at large by assiduous practice in memorizing poetry, the names above shop doors in the street, the positions of playing-cards on a table, sections of the dictionary, and so on. The fallacy of this belief can be illustrated by reference to an experiment, reported in the *British Journal of Psychology*, by W. G. Sleight in 1911. His subjects were eighty-four school girls whose average age was 12 years and 8 months. At the start of the experiment, each girl was given ten different learning tests. These tests involved: memorizing dates of historical events, lists of nonsense syllables, stanzas of poetry, passages of prose, and lists of names; immediately reproducing the gist of a factual prose passage, the positions of towns and rivers on a map, a dictation passage, an array of visual forms, and a list of letters of the alphabet. The performance of each girl on these 'fore-tests' was scored. On the basis of this score, she was allocated to one of four groups, so that each group, as a whole, had done equally well on the fore-tests. Three of those four groups were then given practice in memorizing. This practice was continued for thirty minutes daily on each of four days per week and for a total of six weeks, that is, for an actual practice time of twelve hours in all. Group I practised memorizing poetry. Group II practised memorizing quantitative facts such as numerical conversion tables, scientific formulae, and geographical distances. Group III was given selections of scientific, geographical, and historical prose passages and required to write out the gist of these immediately afterwards. The fourth group – the Control – had no special practice of any kind.

At the end of the six weeks, each of the four groups was given 'after-tests' comprising the same ten tests as originally given. The actual content of these tests was, of course, different, but they had the same general form, and each test was so constructed as to be equivalent in difficulty to the corresponding test given at the start of the experiment. The interest of the investigation lay in discovering whether the girls would, as a consequence of practice, do better on the after-tests of learning than on the fore-tests. Would they learn more quickly ? But there was the possibility that, quite independently of their training, their learning abilities might have improved as a result of all the other activities in which they had engaged over the six weeks. It was for this reason that the Control Group was included, being given the fore- and after-tests without any memorizing practice in between. In assessing the effects of practice on, say, Group I, Sleight could not simply compare this group's performances on the after-tests with its performances on the fore-tests. These two sets of performances may have differed in consequence of innumerable factors which had nothing whatever to do with the intervening practice as such. It was necessary to compare the performances of Group I on the after-tests with those of the Control Group on the same after-tests. Since the two groups were equated for learning abilities to start off with, and since the major difference between them lay in the presence or absence of practice, any difference in their final learning performances could then be attributed to the effects of practice. This inclusion of a control group was, incidentally, only one of the many careful precautions which had to be taken in order that such a complex study as this should yield completely unambiguous results.

The outcome of Sleight's experiment was a complete absence of any general improvement in learning as a result of any of the three forms of practice. Some of the tests showed a very slight improvement and others showed a slight impairment but, in all tests, the effects were small and not statistically significant. This was true even for the memorizing of poetry in Group 1. After six weeks of practice, these children, relative to the Control Group which had had no such practice, showed no improvement whatever in the poetry after-test. The only exception was that the groups which had practised memorizing poetry and 'tables' showed a significant improvement in the memorizing of nonsense syllables – an improvement which was due to the technique, acquired during training, of organizing the material into rhythmical units.

The conclusion of this and of other similar experiments is clear. Special practice in memorizing does not effect a general improvement in ability to learn. Wherever there is any improvement, it is extremely specific in nature. Thus, practice in memorizing poetry may improve our ability to learn new poems written in the same style: but it does not, of necessity, improve our ability to learn poems in general, for there may be no effect with poems written in a somewhat different style on a different theme. All this gives emphasis to the point that learning is not a unitary ability to be strengthened by mental gymnastics in the way that our arm muscles are strengthened by regular exercises with dumb-bells. We do not have a single over-all learning ability, but rather a large number of more specific abilities, and practice in one no more effects improvement in another than finger exercises make it easier for us to wiggle our toes.

The prospect for improving learning is not, however, as bleak as the above conclusion might suggest. Consider the following interesting little finding. One investigator showed that, with school-children, the teacher's routine insistence on the writing of neat arithmetic papers failed to effect the slightest improvement in the neatness of language and spelling papers: yet if the teacher stressed, during the arithmetic lesson, the general principle of neatness in all working, improvements resulted in the papers of other school subjects even though the topic of neatness was scrupulously avoided in connexion with these other subjects. This illustrates a finding which emerges again and again from the study of learning. It shows that intelligent teaching of general principles can achieve what unenlightened drill does not. If we engage in routine memorizing, we pick up learning techniques which are suited to the very specific type of material learned. But these useful techniques are not transferred to the learning of other types of material. However, if, during practice, someone instructs us in the general principles involved in these learning techniques, might not this assist us when we turn to other kinds of learning ? That it well might was demonstrated by an American psychologist, H. Woodrow, in 1927.

The design of Woodrow's investigation followed closely on that of Sleight. He divided 182 university students into three groups and gave each group a set of fore-tests and after-tests. These tests involved memorizing stanzas of poetry and passages of prose, reproducing the gist of factual prose selections, learning the English meaning of Turkish words, learning the dates of historical events, and finally, a test of auditory memory span for consonants. The Control Group did only the fore- and after-tests. The Practice Group devoted a total of three hours (in eight periods spaced over four weeks) to memorizing poems and nonsense syllables. The Training Group divided this same time of three hours between exercises in memorizing poems and syllables and the receiving of instructions in methods of efficient memorizing. For a total of seventy-six minutes, they listened to an exposition of the techniques of memorizing, including rules and illustrations of how these rules should be applied. They spent the remaining 104 minutes in memorizing poetry and nonsense syllables with the explicit purpose of attempting, as far as possible, to apply the rules they had been given. In the after-tests, the Practice Group was no better than the Control: their learning abilities had not improved as a result of their practice. The Training Group, on the other hand, definitely surpassed the other two groups in every single test – even although it had spent less time in actual memorizing activity than had the Practice Group.

The rules taught to the Training Group were as follows: be alert, concentrate on learning, and have confidence in your ability to memorize; learn by wholes rather than by parts; use recitation; organize the material in terms of its rhythm and its meaning and, with nonsense syllables, of elaborating 'secondary associations'. (The use of repetition was not emphasized because the practice conditions were such that the student had no opportunity for varying the number of repetitions.) These methods were explained, illustrated by reference to examples of poetry and nonsense syllables, and the students urged to use them in their memorizing practice. Notice that the students had no direct practice in applying these methods to the learning of Turkish-English vocabularies, dates of historical events, lists of consonants, or the substance of factual passages. Yet, in the after-tests, the students successfully applied the methods to these unpractised forms of learning. As the Practice Group showed, mere routine practice in memorizing is insufficient to establish techniques which can be used in new learning situations. It is necessary that the students be aware of these techniques in terms of general principles or rules. It has also been found in other investigations that the mere knowledge of rules is, by itself, of no value, unless the individual exerts the effort of putting them into practice. He must learn not only that rules can be used but also how to use them. This latter aspect of improvement is, of course, something which only the individual can achieve for himself. However skilfully rules may be taught, it is, in the last analysis, the individual himself who must learn to apply them through his own intellectual efforts. As was once irreverently remarked about a famous American women's college: you can lead a girl to Vassar but you can't make her think. Nor can you force her to apply the flexible rules of learning.

In summary of this section, it may be said that practice in memorizing is useless as a method of improving learning in general. It is also necessary to understand something of efficient methods of learning and then gain practice in applying these methods to our everyday learning activities.

3. MNEMONIC SYSTEMS*

It is true to say that there are as many mnemonic systems as there are mnemonists. But despite their endless variety, it is feasible to place each system into one of three categories, namely, the visual-symbol type, the digit-letter type, and the successive-comparison type. These three types may now be outlined.

Visual-Symbol Systems. The earliest system on record is that devised, around the year 500 B.C., by the Greek poet Simonides. According to Cicero, the outline of this system occurred to Simonides under dramatic circumstances. A certain Greek had won a wrestling victory at the Olympic Games and was giving a banquet at his house by way of celebration. After the fashion of the times, he invited a poet – Simonides – to provide a recitation as part of the entertainment. After delivering his eulogy, Simonides was called away to speak with two men who were waiting outside, and scarcely had he left than the floor of the banquet room collapsed, killing the host and all his guests. Naturally, relatives wished to sort out the bodies, but these were so mutilated as to be unrecognizable. However, Simonides had observed, during his recital, the positions occupied by the guests in the room and, by searching in the appropriate places, he was able to identify the bodies. He could recall who was present by recalling where they were. This incident set Simonides thinking. If such were the case with places and people, surely names, objects, and even ideas could be better memorized by assigning them fixed positions in space. He would imagine, as vividly and with as much detail as possible, a room. And each item he wished to learn he would visualize as being placed in a certain part of this room. The first item would always be placed, say, on the middle of the far wall, the second on the top left-hand corner of the window, and so on. Then, when he wanted to recall these items, he would systematically peruse this imaginary

---

* This section is condensed from part of an article published in Penguin *Science News* 39 (1956), where further details of these systems, and references to the literature, will be found.

room and find each item located in its particular position. Simonides found that a technique of this sort was, indeed, of considerable assistance in memorizing. He reduced his technique to a system and appears to have taught it to others since both Quintilian and Cicero confess themselves indebted to it. These orators used to prepare their speeches by thinking of each division in connexion with a specific, visualized locality. Since the order of these localities was well known, the speaker had only to imagine each in turn to recall or reintegrate the divisions in their correct sequence.

For obvious reasons, this type of system was called the 'locality' or 'topical' system. (The word 'topical' comes from the Greek word for 'a place'. It is of interest that we still speak of 'topics' in connexion with discourses and that Simonides' system is believed by some to have furnished the origin of such expressions as 'in the first place'.) Since the time of Simonides, many mnemonists have employed variations of the locality system. Rooms, houses, public buildings, the human body, the back and palm of the hand – all of these have been broken up into distinctly visualized localities so that items to be learned in sequence can be associated with them.

In the mid seventeenth century, a Cambridge man, Henry Herdson, devised what might be regarded as a logical development of the locality system. Up to this time, mnemonists had represented sequence by standard visual images occupying different parts of an imagined spatial whole. What Herdson did was simply to dispense with the spatial aspect of the model and employ merely the images themselves. He represented each numeral by one of a variety of objects as follows. 1 = candle, or any elongated object; 2 = swan, or any 2-shaped object; 3 = trident, or any tripartite object; 4 = dice, or any object with four parts; 5 = hand, or any object with five parts; 6 = tobacco pipe, or any 6-shaped object; 7 = open razor, or any 7-shaped object; 8 = spectacles, or any object involving two round shapes; 9 = burning glass, or any 9-shaped object; and 0 = orange, or any round object. An intending mnemonist would decide for himself which particular object would represent each numeral. He would, incidentally, be likely to represent each numeral by only one object: Herdson's system is atypical in using more than one object for each digit. Having made his choice, he would then familiarize himself thoroughly with his code. At this point, he would be in a position to employ his system in exactly the same way as a locality system proper. He need not, of course, limit himself to the first ten numbers. He could extend his code indefinitely. In practice, most mnemonists seem to extend their systems to cover numbers up to thirty and often up to a hundred. Neither need he be bound to any particular code. He is free to represent any number by any visual image he cares to select. The very variety of images used by different mnemonists argues that there is nothing magical about Herdson's selection. One symbol seems to be as appropriate as any other, and it matters little which is used. What is important is that one definite code should be decided upon and should be made completely familiar before being put into use.

This type of system, then, involves the representation of sequence by a succession of predetermined visual symbols. It is these symbols which are associated with the items to be memorized. In so far as mnemonists have offered advice on this all-important associating part of their procedure, it is simply this: first, visualize the two objects together as vividly as possible; and second, never compare more than two items at a time. Suppose Herdson's symbols are being used and it is wished to memorize, in order of size, the largest cities in the world. From largest to smallest, the first three cities are London, New York, and Tokyo. London's position might be fixed by visualizing Big Ben surmounted by a candle around which thousands of people are clustering for warmth. A great flock of swans might be imagined waddling amid the sky-scrapers of New York and trailing havoc in its wake. Three slant-eyed Japanese might be seen perched on an elaborately carved three-legged stool. Each object is visualized as concretely as possible: the candle is a particular candle with distinct individual features. Further, the paired objects are not merely juxtaposed. They are brought into a definite relation with each other, and the more ridiculous, far-fetched, and 'striking' this relation, the better. Once the two objects have been thus visualized together, the mnemonist is free to attend to the next pair. It is unnecessary for him to attempt to keep the first pair of objects in mind while dealing with the second. In fact, any effort to attend to more than one pair at a time is detrimental to memorizing. The rule, often cited by mnemonists, is: never compare more than two items at a time.

The above two pieces of advice, on visualizing and comparing, are so frequently implicit in the writings of different mnemonists that they must be assumed sound. And, for what it is worth, the writer has tried out these rules for himself and become convinced of their utility. Practice is, of course, essential for the effectiveness of these, as for any, techniques. With practice, it becomes a simple matter to visualize two objects clearly and bring them together in a lively and dramatic way. It becomes easy, too, to dismiss this scene from awareness and attend fully to the next pair. There are, however, some people for whom such an accomplishment would never become easy. As we saw in the previous chapter, there exists that minority for whom vivid visual imaging is an impossible task. For them, any system of the visual-symbol type would be totally ineffective. Some of them might even find it inconceivable that such a system could be employed by anyone at all.

In the practical application of the visual-symbol system, mnemonists do not seem to rely exclusively on visual relationships. The examples which they give of their associations reveal that the key object is often related to the given object in verbal terms as well. Consider the task of associating 'Tokyo' with 'three-legged stool'. In addition to visual relations, the Japanese might be thought of as wearing toques, as having a toe stuck in a bottle of Tokay wine, and as crying 'Oh my toe is stuck in the Tokay, oh!'. Here the two items are related together in an imaginary situation which has verbal as well as visual characteristics. Examples employing both means of relating are not at all infrequent in the literature, and it seems that mnemonists are shrewd enough not to pass over any helpful device in the interests of preserving the purity of their chosen system. A system dictates, as it were, the strategy. The tactics it leaves to the individual mnemonist.

In leaving the visual-symbol system, it should be said that it is not only the earliest and most elaborate of the systems:

it is also much the most popular and, after the time of the Greeks, seems to have been in constant use since the early fifteenth century.

Digit-Letter Systems. The second type of system is explicitly designed to assist the memorizing of digit sequences. It was in the year 1684 that von Winckelmann, a German, published his 'most fertile secret' of symbolizing digits by letters of the alphabet. These letters were then built up into easily learned words or sentences. In the following century, variations on von Winckelmann's system appeared, including a version by the philosopher Leibniz. But the system seems to have gained its greatest popularity in the nineteenth century. By way of illustration, one of these systems of a century ago may be cited in detail. It is that devised by an English clergyman and schoolmaster called Brayshaw. His code was as follows.

1	2	3	4	5	6	7	8	9	0	00
B	D	G	J	L	M	P	R	T	W	St
C	F	H	K		N	Q		V	X	
			S			Z				

Applying his system to education rather than to theatrical entertainment Brayshaw published, in 1849, his *Metrical Mnemonics*, which contained a collection of rhymes embodying over 2,000 dates and numerical facts drawn from history, geography, physics, astronomy, etc. These rhymes were clearly intended for use in schools and were, presumably, learned by the pupils of Keighley Grammer School where Brayshaw was headmaster. The method of this facile rhymester is apparent in the following typical example which gives the 'dates' of English sovereigns.

1066 By *men*, near Hastings, William gains the crown:
1087 A *rap* in Forest New brings Rufus down.
1100 Gaul's *coast* first Henry hates, whose son is drowned;
1135 Like *beagle*, Stephen fights with Maude renoun'd.
1154 A *cloak*, at Becket's tomb, sec'nd Henry wears:
1189 And *brave* first Richard oft Saladin dares.
1199 John's *act at* Runnymede England pleased avows:
1216 His *face, in* Parliament, weak third Henry shows.

The verse continues in this way up to the last line which gives the date of Queen Victoria's accession.

1837 Lastly, *our hope* rests on Victoria's will.

Thus, Brayshaw inserts in each line the sovereign's name, some outstanding fact about him, and the date of his accession to the throne. This date is embodied in the second word or in the second and third words combined, it being understood that the dates begin at the year 1000.

None of the other versions of the digit-letter system differ from Brayshaw's in more than three minor respects. First, they may use a different code, e.g. 'one' may be represented by P or W or any other letter of the alphabet. Second, the letters may not be formed into words but may be used initially to construct a phrase in which each successive word begins with the appropriate letter. Thus, 1855, the date of Lord Raglan's death, is represented by the letters C–R–L–L. Instead of embodying these letters in a word such as 'carol–l', they may be embodied in a phrase such as 'Courageous Raglan Lamented Lies'. The third variation concerns, again, the code itself; phonic elements may be used in place of letters. Here each number is represented by a sequence of sounds. Such a system would obviously be preferred by those mnemonists who possess strong auditory imagery.

It should be apparent that these digit-letter systems would, like visual-symbol systems, gain greatly in efficiency by being practised. It is, however, noteworthy that they have played no appreciable role in the stage performances of mnemonists. This is doubtless due, in part, to the lesser interest shown by audiences in an ability to recall numbers as opposed to sequences of objects. But chiefly it may be attributed to the greater difficulty of fitting the letters together into words or phrases. It is impossible to compare only two items at a time: four or five letters at least must be related together simultaneously. Accordingly, this type of system lends itself but poorly to the rapid-fire conditions of the stage. It has, instead, been employed by educators who could take leisure to devise the happy phrase which others could learn and 'decode' as occasion demands. This raises the question of whether Brayshaw was correct in assuming that his was the most effective method of teaching a large body of numerical data. It must be borne in mind that his educational programme involved vast amounts of rote memorizing. His unfortunate pupils had to learn hundreds of dates and distances, to say nothing of the areas and populations of countries. Faced by such an undertaking, pupils may well have found their metrical mnemonics of assistance. The modern pupil, however, would not find it worthwhile to master a digit-letter system since, for good or ill, the educational emphasis has swung away from rote memorizing. School history, for example, is no longer synonymous with lengthy lists of dates.

Successive-Comparison Systems. About the third and last type of mnemonic system little need be said since it has, in part, already been described. This type lacks the formal structure of the other two in that it does not involve the initial mastery of any code. It might even be debated whether it should be classified as a system at all. In discussing Simonides' system, reference was made to the rule: Never compare more than two items at a time. The third system is, in essence, an exploitation of this rule. In memorizing a list of words, the mnemonist compares the first word with the second, bringing them together into some related whole. He then dismisses this whole from awareness and attends to comparing the second and third words. This done, he relates the third word with the fourth, and so on. The important thing is that at no point is he concerned with more than two words: he relates each pair successively. The first word in the series must, of course, be learned as it stands. But, in recall, this word reintegrates the second which, in its turn, is recalled as linked with the third. The actual method of relating any two words together is highly variable. They may be brought together by any of the myriad relationships which used to be described so minutely by philosophers of the British Associationist School. The objects for which the words stand may be visualized together: the words may rhyme; they may suggest some causal sequence of events, either mundane or absurd; they may be related through one or more intermediate words or 'secondary associations'. These are but a few of the ways in which associations might be forged. As with other systems, the mnemonist becomes, with practice, increasingly skilful in relating one item with another.

This successive-comparison system seems to have been used mostly with lists of unrelated words. But it could obviously be employed in the learning of any sequential material. It could, for example, be used in applying the visual-symbol system to the memorizing of digit sequences. As the mnemonist hears each digit, he could visualize its visual symbol and associate this with the symbol representing the following digit. However, in spite (or perhaps because) of the wide applicability of this third system, it seems to have enjoyed little popularity among mnemonists. It appears to have been used more as a device to facilitate the application of the other two systems than as a system in its own right.

4. ORGANIZING

The mnemonic systems just outlined enable their users to perform remarkable feats. But these feats are of a very restricted sort, namely, the rapid memorizing of sequences of unrelated items. This being so, the systems are entertaining rather than of practical use. Our adult learning is concerned predominantly with the mastery of meaningful material and the small amount of blindly associative memorizing which we undertake does not justify the effort of acquiring a mnemonic system. In childhood, it is true, we are required to memorize much that is, of necessity, meaningless to us. In order to lay the foundations for later learning and living, the child must memorize the sounds, meanings, and spellings of words, the facts of history and geography, the multiplication tables, and so on. But mnemonic systems are, again, of little use to him because their mastery is, if not altogether beyond his abilities, so expensive in time and effort as to be not worth while. It is better, in the long run, that the child slowly and repetitiously memorize what he has to than that he should even more slowly master a mnemonic system which is of no value in itself. But although the formal mnemonic systems are virtually useless in practical life, a consideration of them is by no means un-rewarding, because they emphasize, yet once more, a principle of the first importance. They show what can be achieved by, in a word, organizing. And it is in terms of organizing that our own everyday learning is susceptible to improvement.

There are two facets of the organizing process. The first is the understanding, the making sense of the material to be learned. We have already seen that the more meaningful the material is to the individual, the more easily it is learned. We have also seen that material is meaningful to the extent that it fits into a framework of accumulated past experiences. The material, in other words, derives its meaning from a schema to which it can be readily assimilated. What the mnemonist does is to build up such a schema into which he fits unfamiliar items. That the establishing of schemata is of assistance to later learning is manifest throughout the whole realm of human activity. It can be seen in the performance of the mnemonist. It is seen in the increasingly more rapid learning of the school-child. It is seen in the rapidity with which the specialist, as contrasted with the novice, masters new findings in his chosen field of interest. That the possession of a body of knowledge makes it easier to learn new material which can be related to it is a fact of major importance, and only one further specific example of it need be given here. When Bousfield and Barry studied Mr Salo Finkelstein, they discovered that he had a digit memory span of twenty as contrasted with the average adult span of about seven. His familiarity with figures was such that, for him, digit sequences 'made sense'. He imme-diately perceived them as mathematical functions such as powers, roots, logarithms, and prime numbers, as telephone numbers, historical dates, and so on. And if an occasional number had no immediate familiarity, it acquired distinctive-ness by very virtue of being unusual. As compared with the average person, his performance with numbers is comparable to that of a linguist who understands some foreign tongue which another man does not. In brief, then, the first necessity in efficient adult learning is to relate the material to what is already familiar, to start by surveying and understanding what is to be learned. And, of course, the wider our range of past experience and the greater the variety of our already completed learning, the easier it becomes for us to learn yet more and more new material because of the richness of the 'cabinet' into which it may be 'filed'.

It often happens that, as it stands, the material to be learned cannot be assimilated to schemata. This is especially the case in learning a vocabulary of some foreign language, a list of unrelated words, a person's name, or in any other situation where the material is relatively meaningless to us. It may also happen that, although we have accomplished the first step of understanding the material in a broad sense, it is too bulky or too complex to be easily learned with a view to later recall. This occurs in the learning of history, medicine, law, or any other academic or professional body of information. In the foregoing situations, the second facet of organizing becomes important. The material itself must be reorganized or, to use the vocabulary of 'information theory', recoded in order that it may be either reduced in bulk or more easily related to what is already familiar. Our preceding discussion of mnemonic systems was pregnant with instances of such reorganization and we may now discuss, in outline, the principal forms which it may take.

Suppose an unfamiliar word or name is to be learned. Its learning is facilitated if it can be reorganized to resemble something which is already familiar. Thus, the names Fontenoy, Corunna, and Quatre Bras might be made familiar through the similarity of their sound to 'funny boy', 'cow running', and 'quart of brass'. By means of these homophonic analogies, the unfamiliar is related to the familiar. Many of us employ just this device in learning people's names if these are foreign or strange. Certainly, the writer has found the device of use in this situation although, on occasion, a carelessly contrived analogy may lead to amusing errors as when he once recalled the name Wolfenden (Wolf-in-den) as Foxinlair. When it is a question of relating two items together, similarities in sound may again be used, although many other sources of similarity can also be exploited. For example, if there is difficulty in learning the difference between stalactite and stalagmite, this difference can be clarified by noting that the former grows from the ceiling and the latter from the ground. Here, the common characteristic is, depending on how we view it, a sound or a letter. Again, the port and starboard of a ship may be related to left and right respectively by noting that the words 'port' and 'left' both contain four letters. And again, it can be remembered that 'schema' is singular and 'schemata' plural by noting that both words contain two *a*'s when the former is rephrased as 'a schema'. In these examples – and the reader can doubtless think of many more – one item is related to another by some characteristic which each has in common. However, the two items often have no such common characteristic, and in this case use may be made of a third 'intermediate' or 'secondary' item. This device of using an intermediate is frequently used in learning the vocabulary of a foreign language. Thus, the German words *Stuhl*, *Blume*, and *Koffer* can be related to their English equivalents of chair, flower, and suitcase through the intermediates of stool, bloom, and coffer, respectively. Obviously, it is possible to use more than one intermediate. For example, if 'thirteen' were to be related to 'bath', we could employ two intermediates as follows: thirteen-lucky-dip-bath.

It is sometimes objected that the mnemonic devices just described are ineffective, not to say dangerous, since we sometimes recall the device but not the items it was intended to relate together. However, such an argument overlooks the point that where the device has not helped, it need not necessarily have hindered. The chances are that if we did not learn with the device we would not, in the absence of greater effort, have learned without it anyway. The instances of failure seem to be more than offset by the successes, and the author is not unique in possessing innumerable little items of knowledge which he would never have acquired except by the assistance of some mnemonic device. It is also, of course, to be noted that the device does no more than forge the first contrived relationship between the items, and that when the direct relation between them has been strengthened by repetition, the device has served its purpose and is often forgotten.

The above discussion has outlined, in a general way, the commonest techniques for relating two items together. Only a few illustrative examples have been given because instances of such techniques are legion in real-life learning, although perhaps most of us do not make quite as much use of them as we might. It may, however, be valuable at this juncture to mention how these reorganization techniques can be used in the familiar, and sometimes troublesome, situation of learning 'names and faces'. The general procedure is simple. We have already seen that the first necessity is to accept each new introduction as a learning challenge. The second necessity is to look for those distinctive aspects of the name and the face which will enable us to relate them together. The name must, of course, be got right even if we have to ask for it to be said again. We must ask ourselves if the name is strange or if it is the same as that of someone we already know. We must examine its peculiarities and also some of the many associations which these peculiarities suggest. And as with the name, so with the person's appearance. What does he look like ? Anyone we know ? An animal or bird perhaps ? What are his outstanding characteristics ? The material must then be organized. Relations must be found between the name and its owner, and the more bizarre these relations the better, even if they are uncomplimentary to the object of our scrutiny. With a little practice, this entire procedure of relating name and face takes much less time to perform than it has taken to describe. The last necessity is that the association between the person and his name should be given the advantage of repetition. In conversation, we should address our new acquaintance by name as often as polite convention permits. This, then, is the technique. If the reader is not already familiar with it, he should try it out; he will be surprised how effective it is.

This description of how to learn 'names and faces' brings out a further characteristic of organizing, namely, that it not only presupposes but also provides a technique of selective observation. Wherever we deliberately set out to organize or reorganize material to be learned, we inevitably furnish ourselves with a set to observe the salient features of the material, to attend to certain aspects of it and ignore irrelevances and distractions. Thus, selective observing, already mentioned as an essential for efficient learning, emerges almost as a by-product out of our attempts to understand and reorganize the material in question. Indeed, selective observing can be considered not as a separate factor in learning but rather as an integral part of the organizing process. We cannot simply undertake to observe: we must know what to look for and what to ignore, and this can be achieved only to the extent to which we try to understand or reorganize the material to be learned.

When it is more than two items which have to be related together, further reorganizing devices emerge. A common trick is to reorganize the items so that they are embodied in a poem or jingle of some sort. We are probably all familiar with the rhyme which starts off: 'Thirty days hath September; April, June, and November.' It is by means of this verse that many of us learned, and still recall, the number of days in each month of the year. This device exploits all the organizational advantages of rhyme and rhythm and its success is attested by the myriad verses (including Brayshaw's) which have been composed to help us learn the more cumbersome facts of history, foreign languages, and so on. An advantage is often to be gained not only by recasting the material into verse form but also by arranging the lines of the verse in such a way that the first or last letters or words of each line constitute, when taken in sequence, a familiar letter or word combination such as a name or a sentence. This is the time-honoured device of the acrostic, and it is at least as old as the 119th Psalm. This ancient composition consists of twenty-two eight-verse sections corresponding to the twenty-two letters of the Hebrew alphabet. The first word of every verse in each section always begins with the same letter: the letter for the first section is 'aleph', for the second section 'beth', and so on. As most frequently employed, however, the acrostic is not usually in verse form but simply relates the different items altogether in a whole which is either a word or a phrase. A very simple example of this was met with in discussing digit-letter mnemonic systems. Thus, once the number 62174 has been translated into the letters M–D–C–P–S, these are reorganized into a word such as 'madcaps'. Another example is that we must be 'careful' to pronounce the letters c, r, f, and l at the end of French words. And yet another example of this acrostic device is one which is known to many medical students. There are six major infectious diseases which produce a rash, one producing it on the first day after infection, another on the second day, another on the third, and so on. To ease his task of memorizing the incubation period of each disease, the student learns the sentence: 'Very sick people must take no exercise.' The position of each word represents the day on which the rash appears, and the first letter of each word is the same as that of the infection – except in the case of 'no' which indicates, properly enough, that no infection produces rash on the sixth day.

Even where the quantity of material is so large that a comprehensive poem or acrostic is out of the question, it is still possible to facilitate learning through reorganization. Those parts which are similar can be grouped together so that the material assumes a definite outline. It is this logical re-organization to which we are usually referring when we say that some lecture or book presents its material well. In the well-delivered lecture, items of information are not mentioned merely in the order in which the lecturer happens to recall them. The lecturer goes over his material beforehand; he groups and sub-groups those items which are, in some important respect, similar; he develops a sequence of themes each of which leads on logically to the next; he evolves a structured whole into which the parts fit readily and in terms of which those parts cohere in a meaningful way. Thus does the lecturer in preparing a good lecture. Thus also does the conscientious author in writing his book: he knows that easy writing makes for difficult reading. And thus too might we when, say, studying for an examination. In such study, it is neither necessary nor desirable that we should attempt to memorize chunks of text-books and lecture notes. Nor is it sufficient merely to browse through the material, as we might a novel, and hope that it will be assimilated in the way that ink is soaked up by blotting paper. Rather, we should attempt to explore, understand, and evaluate the matter, actively relate it to what we already know, and reorganize it in our own way and in our own words until it becomes, as it were, an integral part of ourselves. Not until the material has been assimilated in this way can we either expect to remember it or be able to make further use of it.

The task of reorganizing may be difficult, and just what form of reorganization is sought varies with the material to be learned, with the individual's past history of learning, and with his present interests. But there are two counts on which reorganizing is worth the labour involved. First, while we are seeking out similarities and differences, we are all the while learning the material, increasing our understanding of it and our familiarity with it. This direct effect of reorganizing on learning is recognized in the saying that there is no better way to learn than to have to teach others. All teachers and most parents know that there has been some topic which they felt they understood – until the time came when they had to present it in simple terms to some inquisitive child and found that their understanding was far from profound. Second, once we have achieved a satisfactory reorganization, we now have a body of information which is both easier to learn and easier to refer to because each part is integrated into a coherent whole instead of being in isolation. There have been many investigations to show that whereas fragmentary detail and isolated facts are rapidly forgotten, they are remembered longer if presented in a coherent statement. The outline or précis of the whole is easily learned and, in later remembering, furnishes us with a framework which can be filled out with appropriate detail, a framework in terms of which parts can be more surely reconstructed than if they had to be recalled on their own.

An extreme example of logical reorganization is that which reduces the actual bulk of the material to be learned by 'eliminating redundancy'. Suppose we want to remember how far an object has fallen through space when it has been falling freely for a given time. We could memorize all the individual distances: after one second, the object has fallen 16 feet, after two seconds, 64 feet, after three seconds, 144 feet, and so on. However, this is a cumbersome and quite unnecessary undertaking. We are ignoring the fact that these numbers are not independent of each other, that there is, to use 'information theory' language, a redundancy in the series. And this redundancy can be eliminated by reorganizing the figures into the statement that the distance fallen at the end of t seconds is $gt^2/2$ feet. Since the value of g is approximately 32, all that need be learned is the simple formula $16t^2$. Having learned this, we have, in effect, memorized thousands upon thousands of individual measurements. We have reduced the bulk of our material enormously and so made learning correspondingly easier. This example illustrates what is meant by the device of eliminating redundancy through reorganization – a device which is basic to all the powerfully simple rules, laws, principles, and generalizations of science and scholarship. Scientists are for ever on the alert for redundancies in their data, and these redundancies attain, if they are important enough, the status of scientific laws. The difference between the law and the original material does not lie in the information contained but in the way it is organized: the law packages up the material into smaller bulk.

But it is not only science which can profit by the device of eliminating redundancy. We too can occasionally use it to facilitate our learning. Professor G. Katona, in a book published in 1940 and entitled *Organizing and Memorizing*, gives many instances of how people can benefit by this device, by, as we say, abstracting the underlying principle. In one of his simpler experiments, for example, he presented adult subjects with the following digits.

| 2 | 9 | 3 | 3 | 3 | 6 | 4 | 0 | 4 | 3 | 4 | 7 |
| 5 | 8 | 1 | 2 | 1 | 5 | 1 | 9 | 2 | 2 | 2 | 6 |

One group of subjects was given three minutes to discover the principle involved while another group spent the same time memorizing the digits in groups of three. When both groups are asked to recall the digits three weeks later, 23 per cent of the principle-seekers reproduced them perfectly while none of the memorizers could. This clear-cut difference between the two groups is a direct function of the amount which the two groups had to learn. The memorizers had to learn twenty-four separate numbers and their locations. Those who noticed the redundancy in the digits had only to learn 'start at the bottom line with 5, add 3, then 4, then 3, then 4 and so on alternately until twenty-four digits are obtained in the two equal rows'. In everyday life, we are not likely to have to seek redundancies in lists of digits but there are, nevertheless, numerous situations where time spent in exploring the material with a view to finding redundancies or principles will save untold amounts of learning effort.

We may now attempt a summary answer to the question of how we can improve our memory. This improvement can only be effected through more efficient learning and this, in its turn, cannot be achieved through drill in memorizing but only by the deliberate and fully conscious undertaking of certain flexible procedures. In the broadest terms, those procedures are, first, the organizing and reorganizing of the material to be learned and, second, the organizing of our study effort. Generalizations concerning techniques of distributed practice, learning by wholes, and recitation have been made in Chapter Two. As for the remaining techniques, these are well summarized in a poem written in 1562 by an Englishman, William Fulwood. In the not inept metaphor of his day, he compares memory to a castle of strategic importance in the battle of life and gives directions by which this coveted fortress may be taken into possession. 'Memorie' he writes 'sayeth:

> To him that would me gladly gaine
> These three precepts shall not be vaine.
> The first is well to understand
> The thing that he doth take in hand.
> The second is the same to place
> In order good and formed race.
> The thirde is often to repeat
> The thing that he would not forgeat.
> Adioning to this castell strong,
> Great virtue comes er it be long '

RECOMMENDED FOR FURTHER READING

There exists no single comprehensive work to which the reader can turn for more detailed information on the study of memory, since most of this information is contained in articles scattered throughout the technical journals. However, the following books are recommended as dealing competently with certain topics and providing further references to the literature.

1. Bartlett, F. C. *Remembering*. London: Cambridge Univ. Press, 1932. This book, now a classic, considers the remembering of stories and events. It is rich in penetrating observation but contains some difficult discussion of a theoretical nature

2. Allport, G W., and Postman, L. *The Psychology of Rumor*. New York: Henry Holt & Co., 1947. A readable, non-technical blend of Bartlett's experimental findings with more recent work in the field of social psychology. It discusses the how and why of the spread of rumour.

3. Woodworth, R. S., and Schlosberg, H. *Experimental Psychology*. London: Methuen, 1954. One of the best and most up-to-date books on experimental psychology. Chapters 23, 24, and 25 survey much of the work on memorizing, but are difficult and somewhat arid for the reader with no previous knowledge of experimental psychology.

4. Stern, W. *Psychology of Early Childhood*. London: George Allen & Unwin, 1924 A non-technical book by one of the founders of child psychology. Part v outlines the development of memory in the young child by means of illustrative observations.

5. Morgan, J. J. B., and Lovell, G. D. *The Psychology of Abnormal People*. London: Longmans, 1948. A not-too-technical survey of abnormal psychology. Chapter 8 is devoted to disorders of memory.

6. Freud, S. *Psychopathology of Everyday Life*. London: T. Fisher Unwin, 1914. Contains Freud's readable and ingenious application of psycho-analytic concepts to everyday remembering and forgetting.

7. McKellar, P. *Imagination and Thinking*. London: Cohen & West, 1957. An interesting book containing excellent discussions of imaging.

8. Barlow, F. *Mental Prodigies*. London: Hutchinson's Scientific and Technical Publications, 1951. A non-psychologist describes mental prodigies including famous memory-men and mnemonists.

INDEX

*Some other books on psychology
are described on the
next few pages*

A DICTIONARY OF PSYCHOLOGY

James Drever

R 5

The technical vocabulary of psychology is not in itself an unduly large one, but several other sciences border upon the psychological field and some knowledge of their terms is also necessary. The stimuli which act upon our sense organs are described in physical terms; what happens in the nervous system is relevant and has to be expressed in physiological terms; abnormal behaviour and the clinical description of it and its causes require medical terms. Thus the technical vocabulary actually used by psychologists tends to be rather extensive.

It is the aim of this dictionary to give some help, not merely to the layman, but also to the student, in what has now become an important branch of contemporary science.

'It is commended with confidence as a document relevant not merely to the experimental psychology of former days, but to recent developments in psychometrics, social psychology, psychopathology and industrial psychology.' – *Higher Education Journal*

USES AND ABUSES OF PSYCHOLOGY

H. J. Eysenck

A281

Psychology occupies a somewhat ambiguous place in the world to-day. Its findings are being widely applied in clinics, in industry, in education, and in the armed forces. At the same time, many intelligent people are critical of the alleged laws of human behaviour discovered by psychologists, psychiatrists, and psychoanalysts, and doubtful about the applicability of scientific methods to the study of human beings. In this book, a well-known psychologist has tried to strike a balance, to indicate to what extent the claims made for his science are justified, and to what extent they fail to have any factual basis. Topics dealt with are the testing of intelligence, selection procedures in schools and universities, vocational guidance and occupational selection, psychotherapy and its effects, national differences, racial intolerance, Gallup surveys, industrial productivity, and many others. In each case, psychological findings are submitted to a searching criticism, and a clear distinction made between those uses of psychology where enough is known to support social action, and those abuses where personal opinions rather than experimentally demonstrated fact seem to be involved.

SENSE AND NONSENSE IN PSYCHOLOGY

H. J. Eysenck

A385

There are many topics in modern psychology about which speculation has been rife for hundreds of years. Much has been written on the powers and dangers of the hypnotic trance, the wonders of telepathy and clairvoyance, the possibility of the interpretation of dreams, the nature and assessment of personality, and the psychology of beauty. These early views, while often amusing, have little value because they are not based on scientific facts. In recent years, much experimental evidence has been collected regarding all these topics, but few reliable accounts have appeared which would acquaint the interested layman with these facts and their possible interpretations and implications. This is what the author has attempted to do in this book, by carefully reviewing and sifting the evidence, by frankly, boldly putting forward a definite point of view where the evidence appears to justify it. Throughout the book emphasis is laid particularly on the detailed discussion of the facts, leaving to the reader the decision as to whether the conclusions drawn are justified.

Outline course
Discuss learning
Begin subject matter

FREUD
AND THE POST-FREUDIANS

J. A. C. Brown

A522

Freud and the Post-Freudians explains the main concepts of Freudian psychology and goes on to review the theories of Adler, Jung, Rank, and Stekel. Later developments in the orthodox Freudian school are also discussed, as are those of the American Neo-Freudians and Post-Freudians in England.

This is the first book published in Britain to bring together all these psychological and sociological schools and criticize them, both from the Freudian standpoint and that of the scientific psychologists.

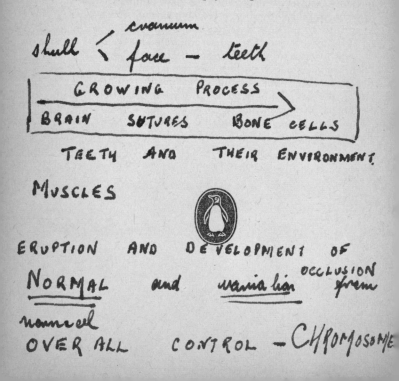

skull < cranium
face — teeth

GROWING PROCESS
BRAIN SUTURES BONE CELLS

TEETH AND THEIR ENVIRONMENT

MUSCLES

ERUPTION AND DEVELOPMENT OF
NORMAL and variation OCCLUSION from
normal
OVER ALL CONTROL — CHROMOSOME